THE OXBRIDGE
REJECT SOCIETY PROSPECTUS

THE OXBRIDGE REJECT SOCIETY PROSPECTUS

Edited by M. W. Buesst and
D. L. Goodhart

Oxbridge Reject Press

A Mandarin Paperback

THE OXBRIDGE REJECT SOCIETY PROSPECTUS

First published in Great Britain 1990
by Mandarin Paperbacks
Michelin House, 81 Fulham Road, London SW3 6RB

Mandarin is an imprint of the Octopus Publishing Group

Copyright © Murray W. Buesst and Daniel L. Goodhart 1990

The right of Murray W. Buesst and Daniel L. Goodhart
to be identified as the joint Authors of this Work
has been asserted by them in accordance with
the Copyright, Designs and Patents Act 1988

A CIP catalogue record for this title
is available from the British Library
ISBN 0 7493 0478 2

Printed and bound in Great Britain
by Cox & Wyman Ltd, Reading, Berks

The Oxbridge Reject Society Prospectus

Edited by M. W. Buesst and D. L. Goodhart

An Introduction
from the Chairman of Governors

*The Oxbridge Reject
Society*

From the Chairman of Governors

Dear Oxbridge Rejects,

It is with the greatest pleasure that I write to
you in this, our Society's seven hundredth year. Seven
hundred years is a long time and it is a tribute to
Rejects, past and present, that we have reached this
milestone so soon.

When our founding fathers first established the
Oxbridge Reject Society for all those who have failed
Oxbridge, they can have had little idea how far it
would journey or how large it would become. Not only
is the Society soon to enter its eighth century, but
last year a greater number of people failed Oxbridge
than ever before, bringing our present membership to
over 250,000, and making us one of the largest
organizations in the country.

As membership of the Society is conferred
automatically, I have no means of knowing exactly who
our 250,000th member is, but I will venture to suggest
that this Unknown Reject fully appreciates why the
Society was created, and is proud to be a member. I am
also sure that he or she feels the same sense of
belonging that unites us all.

But though there is much to celebrate, the war has
yet to be won. I have no doubt that all members of the
Society are as worried as myself about the world in
which we find ourselves. Competition and the pursuit
of excellence are openly being hailed as the solutions
to all our problems. Yet we have all competed, and we

have all pursued excellence - and our common experience
has taught us that embracing these overrated principles
is not entirely without its share of unhappy
consequences. The Society's role in spreading this
message has surely never been so important as it is
today.

I would like to take this opportunity to extend a
very warm welcome to all those new members who have
recently been rejected by the Universities of Oxford
and Cambridge. You should not consider your rejection
to be a reflection on your abilities - we in the
Society realize that the examinations you sat were
simply too difficult, and the grades required of your
simply too high.

You are joining the Society at an historic moment
in its history, and to you, and to all other members of
the Society, I extend my very best wishes for our
eighth century.

I remain your obedient Reject,

Susan Browning

P.P Arthur Botherington
Chairman of Governors,
The Oxbridge Reject Society.

An Oxbridge Reject History
A Paper by the Historical Research Department

Six Hundred Glorious Years:
Oxbridge Rejects and the Shaping of a Nation, 1290–1890

There have been many histories of Great Britain, but even the most famous have been guilty of the sin of omission: Gibbon, Macaulay, and even Trevelyan never referred by name to any Oxbridge Reject. But this is surely no conspiracy of silence; it would be a devious mind indeed that sought to find a connection between these great historians and what they have chosen to ignore. It is undoubtedly nothing more than a coincidence that they all attended the Universities of Oxford or Cambridge.

In truth, I believe that the low profile maintained by members of the Society has been intentional. I would suggest that from the time that Harold was struck by an arrow on the fields of Hastings, it became blindingly obvious that to be in the public eye was to risk an early and violent death. Oxbridge Rejects have, as a result, sought to avoid attention, and it can be seen that in this they have been strikingly successful.

Our research has uncovered much about the Society, as well as about individual Rejects. It has confirmed, for example, that the Society was founded on the 1 April 1290, when a Reject from Oxford University and two Rejects from Cambridge University met in an ale house above a London bakery and established the *Societas Oxtabriensis Rejectorum*. As far as it has been possible to ascertain, meetings of the Society were held in these same premises in Pudding Lane every year until the 376th anniversary celebrations, which were a roaring success until they got out of hand, and the building – and half of London – was destroyed by fire.

The loss of so many of the Society's archives in this fire, and the avoidance of notoriety cultivated by individual Rejects, has made historical research into the influence of Oxbridge

Rejects extremely difficult to conduct. But the hindrances experienced have been more than rewarded by those findings which the project has brought to light. It has become apparent that Rejects have played a very important role in the development not only of the Society to which we belong, but also of the nation in which we live.

The report which follows reveals what has been hidden for so long – those who have been influential but who have been content to live without the trappings of power, glory and a regular income.

As Emerson said, 'There is properly no history – only biography.' This paper looks at the lives of a small number of Rejects who, although long since dead, should not, having been remembered, now be forgotten.

Mathew Donaldson,
Rejectus Professor of Modern History,
The Oxbridge Reject Society

EDITOR'S NOTES
In the early eighteenth century Britain and Europe adhered to the Julian and Gregorian Calendars respectively. To avoid the confusion that this could cause, most dates have been removed from the text.

In accordance with Oxbridge Reject Press policy, this article does not contain a glossary, an index, or any footnotes.

ACKNOWLEDGEMENTS
As with all projects of this size and scope there are a great many individuals and organizations who have helped – in a variety of ways – in its realization.

In particular, I must of course thank the Society for funding the research from which this paper is drawn. When the project was first commissioned it was anticipated that it would take two years. The Historical Research Department has gone somewhat over budget since that day in 1888, but happily successive Treasurers have recognized the importance of our work, and have continued to provide financial support.

I am greatly indebted to my seventeen predecessors who have run the Historical Research Department and worked on the project over the last one hundred and two years. Their individual contributions cannot be evaluated separately – a fact of which some of them seem to have been only too aware – but together I hope that we have produced a work of scholarship that will stand the test of time. The task has been an enormous one, and there can be no doubt that this is the reason that it has never before been attempted.

I am grateful to the staff of the Oxbridge Reject Society Library, where I wrote and edited much of what follows, for their boundless expertise and enthusiasm, and for their help in tracing the Blügen Collection.

I am particularly indebted to the Society's travel fund for making it possible for me to visit Vienna to examine the Blügen Collection. I spent a useful two weeks there, but it was unfortunate that at the time the collection was on loan to the British Library.

I am very grateful to the Danby Trust for allowing me access to the Danby Letters. As agreed, the paper that follows contains no mention of Henry Danby's unusual sexual practices.

The article on Wat Platter has appeared previously in the Czechoslovakian edition of the *Workers' New Marxist-Leninist Revolutionary Economic Review for the Promulgation of Advanced Agricultural Studies* (Vol. 12; No. 764; Feb/March 1949). I am grateful for their permission to reproduce it here.

I would like to thank my nephew, Victor Donaldson, who kindly read the final draft of this paper and made a number of valuable suggestions – all of which I have chosen to disregard.

As always I am indebted to my wife, who corrected the manuscript and final proofs. All typographical, grammatical, stylistic, and factual errors must now be attributed to her.

1. Richard, William, Reginald and Hugh: Oxbridge Rejects?

'Becket's death prevented English novices from travelling to Paris to study for the priesthood, and was therefore directly responsible for the growth of Oxford as a centre of learning after 1170.'

Oxford University, an Episodical History
by Lord Percy Makepeace

When Richard, William, Reginald and Hugh murdered Thomas à Becket on the altar steps of Canterbury Cathedral, they little knew that their action was to lead ultimately to the foundation of the Oxbridge Reject Society, or that they would later be held by some to be its first members.

The political implications of their crime were to prove far-reaching; tensions between the Crown and the Pope rapidly escalated, and it was soon difficult for English scholars to travel to the continent to study. Oxford, until then a religious centre of only secondary significance, gained a new prominence.

The murderous knights, upon realizing the enormity of their mistake, vowed to atone for their actions by devoting themselves to the study of the Word of God. Naturally, it was to Oxford that they travelled in order to begin their lives of repentance. Unfortunately in the twelfth century, as in present times, the murder of an archbishop was a serious crime, and despite being largely responsible for the political climate which had led to Oxford flourishing as a seat of learning (and later as a university), they were not even invited for interview. One possible explanation for this is that in their applications to study for the priesthood each listed under 'recent achievements': 'The execution of the Primate of all England'. They had become Oxford's first four Rejects.

The early Society was rocked by a number of internal disputes about the true nature of rejection. Records show that in 1291, when the Society was only a year old, the four knights became the subject of a heated debate which was to lead to a severe rift. The schismatics argued that the knights should be recognized as the true founders of the Society. This was hotly disputed by those who had been present at the first meeting in 1290 and who argued that until Oxford became a university it was not possible to be rejected in the proper manner. Furthermore, they held that even in the violent times in which they lived, the knights' crime was exceptional and rendered them unfit to be members of the Society. A clause was introduced into the constitution (which remains in force today) stating that anyone who has murdered an archbishop is not eligible for Society membership. As a result of this dispute, the apologists for Richard, William, Reginald and Hugh broke away from the Mother Society and became known for a while as 'knightists'; this sect was later to fizzle out.

It is to be regretted that the Society's origins are linked so closely to an act of violence, but it must be remembered that such barbarity was endemic in the twelfth century. Whilst not wishing to condone the knights' actions, however, it is important not to underestimate their influence in shaping the Society's early years. In addition, as well as playing a key role in the historical circumstances which led to the Society's founding, they also fell victim to the sort of misunderstanding which has beset Oxbridge Rejects ever since.

2. Wat Platter, Oxbridge Reject.

'It was improved agricultural techniques, and in particular the trend towards rotating crops and leaving land fallow, that allowed the population to expand so rapidly in the early fourteenth century.'

The Cambridge Economic History of Europe
by Professor P. J. Milne

Agriculture in the Middle Ages was extremely inefficient by the modern standards of the European Economic Community. Those working on the land could do no more than feed themselves and their families, leaving very little surplus food with which to trade, thereby restricting the growth of markets and the development of towns.

It is not widely realised that this situation was ended by the first second-generation Oxbridge Reject, Wat Platter. Wat was the only son of Robin Platter, a tenant farmer in Staffordshire. Although naturally indolent, Wat had shown some indications of intelligence, and possessed a vivid imagination, so in 1313 his father sent him forth on foot to Cambridge where it was hoped that he would learn something that would be of use in helping to run the family farm. Unfortunately when Wat arrived in Cambridge he was told that, as with his father before him, there was no place available. This was because the course for which Wat had applied, Land Economy, had yet to be introduced.

On returning to Staffordshire, Wat discovered that his father had been called up for the newly-introduced jury service, leaving strict instructions that if he had not returned by the spring, Wat was to plant all crops as usual. Two months later news reached Platter from his father that the trial was still in progress, and concerning as it did a particularly serious crime (that of stealing a loaf of bread), it might well stretch on for many more months. Wat was to plant the crops immediately.

Rather than do this by hand, Wat – regarding himself now as a Cambridge man – resolved to devise a new method which would make his name, and avoid the back-breaking work entailed in manually broadcasting the seed. His first idea was to cast a spell which would cause the plough to till the land and the sacks of seed to distribute themselves evenly across the fields. But despite repeating the incantation at all times of day and night, with a mustard seed in his mouth, and a forked twig in his pocket, the plough and the sacks of seed remained inactive.

The following week Wat was daydreaming at church when he heard voices telling him to leave the seeds out for the birds to distribute. He ran straight home from church to carry out these heaven-sent instructions and was delighted by the huge number of birds that immediately flew to help him in his task.

14

In due course, Wat's father sent word that his jury service was to detain him for a further year, as the severity of the sentence now hinged on establishing the extent to which Exhibit A had been cooked, and therefore whether it should be properly classed as dough, bread or toast. Robin Platter expressed his hopes that the harvest had been good, and reminded Wat to plant the next year's crops.

In fact the experiment of using birds to scatter the seed had not been a great success, and the poor yields had convinced Wat that the traditional method of distribution was, after all, the best. He therefore set about sowing by hand. Unfortunately Wat found it impossible to establish which crops had previously been growing on what land and he was forced to rely on guesswork.

Eventually the trial came to an end and Robin Platter journeyed back to Staffordshire to find his farm in disarray. He was furious to discover that his son had planted turnips where wheat had grown, wheat in place of radishes, and radishes in the turnip field. However, it rapidly transpired that leaving the land fallow and rotating the crops had had a very significant effect on the yields, and a huge harvest of each soon calmed his anger.

Wat Platter's contribution in devising these significantly improved agricultural techniques has not been widely applauded. Previous historians have dismissed his achievement as the result of accident. But this is to overlook the importance which chance has played in many similar scientific revolutions. Platter himself was to make a valuable contribution to the dissemination of his new techniques by writing three extremely influential tracts which were the first books to be published by the Oxbridge Reject Press: *What They Don't Teach You at Cambridge Agricultural College*, *Wat on Earth*, and his autobiographical *The Fallow Fellow*.

3. Sir Gerald Smythson, Oxbridge Reject.

'The Black Death was a turning point in the development of the British Isles for three reasons.'

The Impact of the Black Death
on the Poetry of the Fourteenth Century
by Dr Janice Waverley

Sir Gerald Smythson's name is not well-known today, but in the 1340s in southern England he was much respected. He had won his reputation and a knighthood during the previous decade by importing foot-and-mouth disease into the country in a much applauded attempt to rid the British Isles of wolves. It was therefore natural that the nation should turn to Sir Gerald in 1348 when rumours of a plague sweeping Europe first reached Britain.

Ye Councylle for ye Confounding of ye Dreaded and Most Feared Plague was immediately convened under Sir Gerald's chairmanship. At the time, little was known about the plague except that it had originated in the East. Less still was known about the East except that it was from there that cats came. The connection was clear to Sir Gerald, and he sent out orders accordingly.

Throughout the country, vermin controllers were appointed and equipped with cat-catching equipment. Their task was to use these large wooden boxes to catch all wild and domestic cats and, in particular, all those that lived on ships. In this they were highly effective, and within three months the number of cats throughout the country was approximately halved. But despite these precautionary measures Ye Councylle for ye Confounding of ye Dreaded and Most Feared Plague was not entirely successful in its objectives, and was forced to conclude that rats might have been a more important element in the spreading of the plague than had initially been suspected.

Realizing the mistake that had been made, Sir Gerald sent out further orders. All vermin controllers were now to concentrate on catching rats. Unfortunately recent expenditure on cat-catching equipment prevented the provision of similar apparatus designed for rats, and if these were now to be caught there was only one way to do it: Sir Gerald ordered his vermin controllers to requisition food from all householders and to leave it lying in the streets. Only by feeding rats until they became the size of cats, he argued, could the equipment be of use, and the rat population controlled.

His policy was partially successful. Some rats did grow to be the size of cats, and although at least two vermin controllers died in the process, many of these super-rodents were caught. Unfortunately the majority of the rat population was too busy breeding to grow sufficiently. In contrast, the human population of Britain, having been deprived of food and surrounded by plague-carrying rats, was not in such an enviable position. A third of them died and were therefore unable to join in the celebrations, two years later, which marked the accession of Sir Gerald to the post of Chairman of Governors of the Oxbridge Reject Society. The Archive reports that, 'Sir Gerald Smythson, by ye Grace of God, did live for another two score yeares, and did be a marvlous fyne Chairman indeede.'

Many of Sir Gerald's contemporaries were quick to dismiss his endeavours as 'bureaucraticke bunglynge of ye worst kinde'. But this is to overlook the extent to which his exploits have enriched the English language, thereby improving the quality of the British way of life. It was Sir Gerald who was directly responsible for the introduction of such words as catalogue (a list of vermin controllers), catastrophe (the demise of one third of the population), catering (literally the feeding up of a rat to the size of a cat), irrational (illogical approach to the diagnosis of the origins of a plague), rates (originally the food tax imposed by ye Councylle on property owners), ratify (to vote on measures usually pertaining to the confounding of plagues) and bureaucratic (using a large wooden box or desk to catch feline creatures or rodents).

4. James Squirrel, Oxbridge Reject.

'So oftenne in ye past it has not been ye protagonystes
that have most influenced events but those behynd ye
protagonystes: ye generals, ye bishoppes and ye
lawyers.'

From the Introduction to
Tayles for Children,
by James Squirrel

In 1529, James Squirrel was the senior member of the
Oxbridge Reject Society's Legal Deparment and the author
of a number of children's books. He was also, as it happened,
at the pinnacle of his career.

For some time, Squirrel, considered by many Rejects to
be the finest legal mind of his generation, had been thinking
about new areas of specialization. In April he finally decided
to abandon conveyancing in order to concentrate on divorce
work. At the time, since divorce was almost unheard of,
very few lawyers had any experience in this area, so it was
not long at all before he made a considerable mark.

His first and – as it transpired – only divorce brief was to
arrange the annulment of Katharine of Aragon's marriage,
and Squirrel wasted no time in attempting to devise a
watertight case for his client, Henry VIII. Unfortunately the
King proved to be little better at choosing lawyers than he
did at selecting his wives.

Squirrel initially suggested that Katharine be denounced
as a foreigner. Henry remarked, however, that at the time
of his marriage to the King of Spain's daughter, this fact had
hardly been kept a secret. Having failed to persuade his
Queen to enter a nunnery, Squirrel then suggested that the
King claim to be impotent and argue that his marriage was
never consummated. Henry was deeply offended by this
second suggestion, pointing out that the case might be
somewhat weakened by the fact that Katharine had borne
him seven children and, even though only one had survived,

their daughter Mary could be a rather damaging witness.

At the last minute (and without consulting the King) Squirrel therefore developed a third line of reasoning which he used when the Legate's Court opened in London in May 1529. He argued that Henry had been married to Katharine for eighteen years, which was a very long time, and that now 'he fancyed a change'. This change, Squirrel announced in Court, was Anne Boleyn.

After being imprisoned for two months in the Tower of London, during which time he completed a number of books, including his masterly *Tayles for Children*, Squirrel was beheaded. The following day the Court was adjourned.

The failure of the Legate's Court, resulting largely from Squirrel's inexperience in divorce work, was to have two important consequences: the first was the dismissal from the King's service of the Papal Legate and his closest advisor, Cardinal Wolsey, who was both an Oxbridge graduate and the founder of Christ Church College, Oxford. The second was a further deterioration in relations with the Pope, leading to the Reformation, and subsequently to the Dissolution of the Monasteries, the implementation of which fell to an Oxbridge Reject. This was to prove immensely profitable to the Society's own coffers, having a marked effect on its prosperity right up to the present time.

5. Henry Danby, Esq, Oxbridge Reject.

'There were more than 130 ships in the Armada. With such a force the Spanish believed that they could defeat the smaller English fleet and clear the way for an invasion by their army waiting in the Netherlands.'

Europe in Turmoil: 1588–1988
by Edwin Elderman

Many minority groups faced hostility during the latter half of the sixteenth century, and the Oxbridge Reject Society was no exception. The Society's immense wealth made it unpopular with elements in the royal court, and this culminated in a short spell of persecution under Lady Jane Grey. By the time Elizabeth ascended to the throne, the Society had determined to embark upon a campaign to restore its popularity. One of the ways that this policy was realized was through sports sponsorship.

It was widely reported that Sir Francis Drake refused to attack the Armada until he had finished his game of bowls. It is less well known that bowls was the passion of his life – he regularly played in tournaments and frequently won them.

The Oxbridge Reject Society was the sponsor and organizer of the 1588 All England Bowls Championships. Henry Danby had been appointed Tournament Secretary in 1586, but did nothing to organize the competition until April 1588. By then the greens at the usual venue – Newbiggin-by-the-Sea, near Newcastle – had been booked. Danby could only find suitable facilities at Plymouth. This West Country port offered most of the advantages of Newbiggin: its greens were well maintained and it was usually quiet at the beginning of summer.

Danby's choice was to have a marked effect on the future of England's independence. On the 21 July, Drake, having won nine games in three days, reached the final. He was ahead by fourteen points to ten when the Armada was sighted off the coast of Plymouth. Just three quarters of an hour later, having failed to win the title, Drake was able to embark and launch his attack on the Spanish.

Had Drake been in Newbiggin it would have taken him more than three days to reach the Channel. While Danby's organizational abilities must be credited, so too must his talent as a bowls player. It was Danby who beat Drake in the final. If Drake had won, he had intended to turn professional and to abandon sea-faring altogether.

As it transpired, this was to be the last bowls competition organized by the Society, as its bowls sets were requisitioned by the Royal Navy and used to sink much of the Spanish fleet.

Drake played bowls with Danby on many subsequent occasions, and some years later he introduced the young Reject to his cousin's husband's son, Walter Raleigh, who had recently graduated from Oxford. Danby and Raleigh became very close friends indeed, until a dispute arose between them concerning a velvet cloak that the Reject had lent to his new friend. Danby was killed in the ensuing duel.

6. Tim Brown, Oxbridge Reject.

'The battle of Waterloo was won on the playing fields of Eton.'

Arthur Wellesley, First Duke of Wellington

Wellington recognized that, more than anything else, it is the playing of sport that fosters the skills which bring victory in war. To understand Britain's military success one must therefore look to the games that were played in her schools.

It is generally accepted that the sport that is most effective in instilling comradeship, initiative and discipline is not soccer, rowing or cricket, but rugby. The origins of few games can be traced with such accuracy. It was in 1823 that William Webb Ellis, while playing football at Rugby School, first caught the ball and ran forward with it.

The referee at the time, an Oxbridge Reject Latin teacher, did not realize that anything was amiss until the opposing goalkeeper, Tim Brown, threw himself at Ellis and made the game's first tackle. It remains the contention of the Oxbridge Reject Rugby Football Association that it is from this moment that the modern game has descended. Ellis's catching and running with the ball was significant, but only in that it led to Brown's tackle. It was the tackle that was the more important of the two developments, setting the game apart from all others played at the time.

Science had yet to be included in the curriculum of British schools, and in launching himself into the first tackle, Brown had given little consideration to the combined effects of momentum and gravity. It was a brave attempt, and although it did not stop Ellis from scoring, Brown was lucky to escape with only heavy bruising to his head, sternum, pelvis and legs. Unluckily for Brown, however, it was at this

21

moment that the referee began to realize that something was wrong. He ruled Brown's brilliant initiative 'ungentlemanly behaviour', and sent the boy home for three weeks. When he returned, the new game, complete with tackling, was both famous and compulsory.

William Webb Ellis later applied to Oxford University, and was accepted. He was thought to have shown flair and imagination. Brown was rejected by Cambridge largely as a result of his Latin teacher's report, which suggested that he was abnormally aggressive. Amongst members of the Society's Rugby Football Association it is often seen as paradoxical that while Brown was rejected by Cambridge for inventing the key part of a game that is played all over the world, many students were later to win scholarships to Oxbridge specifically because of their ability to play the same game.

Since Tim Brown made his historic tackle, Britain has not lost a war. Unfortunately Brown himself was to remain ignorant of his long-term contribution to the nation. On leaving Rugby School he joined the Cavalry, and had reached the rank of Major in the Light Brigade when the Crimean War began. He was killed leading a charge against Russian guns.

7. Charlotte and Emily Stephenson, Oxbridge Rejects.

'When George and Robert Stephenson entered their locomotive "Rocket" at the Rainhill trials, it heralded the start of the Railway Age.'

The First Industrial Nation:
Steam Power in Britain, 1829–1914,
by Michael Dobert

The Stephenson sisters are important figures in the Oxbridge Reject Society because they were our first female members. They joined in 1822 when there were, of course, no Colleges at Oxford or Cambridge admitting women. This did not stop Charlotte and Emily from applying, but it may be a factor that would help to explain their rejection.

George Stephenson's three children, Robert, Charlotte and Emily, were all, from a very early age, interested in thermodynamic theory, and particularly in the interplay of enthalpy and entropy within the basic steam engine. George welcomed this interest, and encouraged his children to enter into a protracted correspondence with Sir Humphry Davy and other important scientists of the day. Quite soon, all three children developed a remarkable ability to realize projects of great complexity.

The 'Rocket' was one such project. It was Charlotte and Emily who first suggested that the family should attempt to build a steam-engine. During its construction the girls spoke little about its potential uses, either to George and Robert, or to each other. However, letters show that both girls had envisaged specific applications. Charlotte had thought that the steam-driven 'Rocket' might be used to increase the amount of leisure time available to women, through 'the directed use of steam and pressurized water to carry out the automated washing of dirty crockery'. Emily, on the other hand, had only considered the possibility of 'a mechanical device which would help ladies squeeze into their tight-fitting bodicies'.

Both sisters were very disappointed to discover that George and Robert had entered the engine at the Rainhill trials – without their permission. They were even more upset when they realized that they were directly responsible for greatly accelerating the pace of life in Britain, as first transport and then industry were transformed by the Stephenson Rocket.

While Robert Stephenson continued to work as an engineer, and was later to be given an honorary degree by Oxford University in recognition of his contribution in this area, Charlotte and Emily did not undertake any further engineering projects. Within a few years both were married: to Mr Currer Mills and Mr Ellis Boon respectively. The two couples lived together in Yorkshire, and over the course of the next three decades, Charlotte and Emily wrote one hundred and twelve novels and bore twenty-two children.

The story of the Stephenson steam-engine is not unique. Ideas often develop beyond initial expectations, and large projects are rarely realized strictly as planned. Nevertheless, it is to be regretted that to this day there is still no device, be it steam-powered or otherwise, to help ladies into their undergarments.

8. Mr Edward Compton, Oxbridge Reject.

'Whatever territories still fly the Union Jack, Britain is, and will remain, an Imperial Nation.'

Rule Britannia! Stories from the Empire,
by Lady Blythe-Cooper

At various stages in Britain's history, Rejects have been attracted towards specific professions. When the Society was first established, Rejects were denied the modern option of alternative universities and many entered the Church or the Army, only to discover that these were the two most influential bodies of the day. Having split the Church and precipitated a civil war, Rejects began to realize that these were unnecessarily stressful areas of employment and looked elsewhere.

By the nineteenth century, as the impact of the Industrial Revolution made the pace of life in Britain increasingly rapid, many began to choose careers that would allow them to leave the country. Oxbridge Rejects travelled to every corner of the world and in all guises: as explorers, as administrators, as circus performers and even as missionaries. As explorers they charted new-found territory; as administrators they ruled vast areas of land; as missionaries they converted heathens to Christianity; and sometimes they were called upon to perform a remarkable balancing act between these posts.

Eventually the extent of the Rejects' activities and, in particular, the enormous amount of land being claimed for Her Britannic Majesty, began to attract attention back in Britain. Although it cost little to discover and explore such territory, the land gained was, too often, completely worthless. Furthermore, Parliament was becoming increasingly antagonized by the cost of protecting the Empire, the need constantly to reprint Foreign Office maps, and the chronic shortages of both pith-helmets and cleft sticks for carrying messages.

It is well known that Gladstone wrote letters to British administrators on many continents demanding that the Empire cease to grow. It is less well known that four fifths of these letters failed to reach their destinations, and, as a result, Rejects continued to enlarge the Empire until it included a quarter of the world's land and a fifth of its population. Until very recently it was something of a mystery as to why so many of Gladstone's letters never reached the Colonies.

Like many of his contemporaries in the Society, Edward Compton was a man who dreamt of colonial adventure. To escape from Britain he joined the Imperial Administration section of the General Post Office. After thirty-two years of service, however, he had got no closer to the tropics than Marylebone Sorting Office. It was here, as Acting Second Deputy Assistant to the Chief Postmaster, that Edward Compton was to make his contribution to the British Empire. It had little to do with the advances he pioneered in sorting techniques and much to do with his hobby of philately.

Working for the Post Office, Edward Compton had developed a love of stamps. The postal service was expanding very rapidly at this time, however, and management training in the sector was overstretched. As a result Compton never realized exactly what the little paper squares with the perforated edges were for. Consequently, when he saw stamps that he liked, he removed them from envelopes and kept them for his collection. The letters were therefore never delivered. Gladstone's official correspondence passed through Marylebone Sorting Office, and much of it suffered this fate at the hands of Edward Compton.

Although William Gladstone was responsible for shaping much of British society in the latter half of the nineteenth century, in Edward Compton he had met his match.

25

Compton was eventually arrested, aged fifty-eight as he concluded a lecture delivered to the Knightsbridge and Brompton Women's Institute on 'The Joys of Stamp Collecting'. After a celebrated trial he was imprisoned for two days, and suspended from his job for three weeks. On release from prison he resolved to abandon stamp collecting altogether and his magnificent collection of unfranked Victorian stamps was sold to the Austrian philatelist, Count Leopold von Blügen. It can now usually be seen on display in Vienna.

Whilst Compton spent just forty-eight hours in confinement for his misdemeanours, the consequences of his actions were to last rather longer than this. Gladstone's grand design for Imperial shrinkage was unwittingly foiled, and the Empire grew to be the largest the world has ever seen. The influence of Rejects on such a large proportion of the earth remains with us: indeed there are, today, few people working in the postal sector around the world who are unaware of the purpose of little paper squares with perforated edges.

CONCLUSION

It is the job of the historical to find a consistent pattern in the infinite variety of shifting circumstances, and I believe that the Historical Research Department has found just such a pattern. Attributing the development of a country to just a few individuals is often criticized as being a 'superficial' practice. This, of course, is nonsense. I hope that this paper has done something to answer these critics, and it can now be understood that it is not the basis of the argument that should be questioned, but the choice of the few individuals.

In a task as large as this, much of value has, of course, had to be omitted, and this paper represents little more than a sketch. It is a shame, for example, that there has been no room here to examine the Oxbridge Reject influence behind Britain's free trade policy of 'laissez-faire', or the role played by Charles I's constitutional adviser, or Joan of Arc's defence lawyer.

It has not been easy to condense the Historical Research Department's activities over the last 102 years into these few pages, and I hope that one day we will be given the opportunity to write at greater length about this fascinating subject. Although the present paper has not covered the period since 1890, it should not be supposed that Rejects have become any less influential over the course of the last century. One thinks of the Oxbridge Reject who, when asked by a passing crowd where Jarrow Town Hall was, in order that they might march to it, accidentally pointed them in the direction of London; and of the Reject introduction agency responsible for finding Mrs Wallis Simpson her Prince Charming. There are many such episodes. But the fact is that in our own century, just as in the preceding six, Reject influence has gone largely unnoticed.

Mathew Donaldson,
The Historical Research Department

BIBLIOGRAPHY

There have been several books written on the subject of Britain's development over the last seven centuries. In particular I have made extensive use of the following Oxbridge Reject Press publications:

Donaldson, M.: *Historical Perspectives on Astrology: Taureans in the Franco-Prussian War* (1953)

Donaldson, M.: *The Thirty Years War: the First Bit of the Hundred Years War* (1964)

Donaldson, V.: *Nepotism Through The Ages* (With a foreword by M. Donaldson) (1978)

Kildare, J.: *The Diet of Worms: Nutritional Secrets from the Holy Roman Empire*, (1521)

Gunther, K.: *Power Corrupts: Images of the Political Id*. (1975).

Paste, B.: *Louis XIV: Where Did He Find Time to Make All that Furniture?* (1949)

Pegge, O.F.: *A Statistical Analysis of the Impact of the Glorious Revolution on Roofing Materials in Little Gaddesden* (1964)

Pegge, O.F.: *A Statistical Analysis of the Impact of the Glorious Revolution on Roofing Materials in Great Gaddesden* (1968)

Unsworth, M.: *From Charles De Gaulle to John F. Kennedy: Franco-American Aviation Routes 1976–78* (1979)

The Annual Report
Introduced by the Administrative Supervisor

The Oxbridge Reject Society

From the Administrative Supervisor
Alison Clare, BA Hons (Oxon), MBA (Harv)

In 1979 the Oxbridge Reject Society was a Society in decline.

During the previous decade the Society had lost much of the respect which it had previously enjoyed amongst intellectual circles, as they witnessed the widening gap between capacity and output, the phasing-in of a three-day week (initially as a four-day weekend), and the increasingly widespread view that the Society represented the "unacceptable face of rejection".

In a bid to turn the tide, a respected firm of management consultants was commissioned to report on the Society's departmental structure and find ways to arrest falling productivity. The report's sole recommendation was that an Administrative Supervisor be appointed to oversee the general administration of all ORS departments, that the occupant of this post be head-hunted from outside the Society, and - moreover - that he or she be a graduate of either Oxford or Cambridge University.

Needless to say, the consultants' report was unpopular with some elements within the Society. Many members, however, recognised the urgency of the situation, and finally a compromise was reached whereby the Treasury retained its independence whilst the rest of the Society's departments were placed under the control of an Administrative Supervisor. In 1979 I was chosen to fill that post.

Eleven years on, we are reaching the end of a period of extensive rationalisation of all those activities which fall under my aegis: where synergy was perceived to exist departments have been merged; other operations have been put out to private tender, and the Society orchestra has been disbanded. Productivity has greatly increased, overmanning has been reduced, and deadlines are now frequently met. The medicine has been strong, but it was desperately needed.

But there are still many areas where I expect to see improvements if the ORS is to be ready to enter its eighth century in a competitive spirit of free enterprise. We cannot afford to carry passangers in a streamlined, modern and forward-looking Oxbridge Reject Society. We must face up to reality; if ORS departments cannot learn to pay their way then we will have to learn to live without them.

I look forward to working with you during the next decade. I have no doubt that it will be an exciting and challenging time for us all.

Ms Alison Clare
Administrative Supervisor,
The Oxbridge Reject Society

Notes on the Reports

The Administrative Supervisor writes: I am glad to see that in addition to detailing their year's progress, some Departments have begun to state their overall objectives at the beginning of their summaries. This is a useful discipline in managerial prioritisation.

However, having circulated the acetates from my lecture series, 'Streamlining in the '90s: Effective Management, Marketing and Communication Tools for ORS Departments', I am disappointed to find that department heads are still not using these annual reports as an opportunity to identify their indirect competitors, conceptualise possible areas of diversification, or assess their performance parameters.

The Membership Department's Report

The Membership Secretary writes: The Oxbridge Reject Society has always been one of the most difficult organizations in the world to join. The Membership Department is largely responsible for this fact, since its principle function is to interpret the Constitution in order to lay down the Society's entrance requirements.

There are currently three ways of joining the Society, which apply equally to both undergraduates and postgraduates:

1. Applying to an Oxford or Cambridge College, and receiving a letter of rejection. All candidates fulfilling these criteria qualify automatically, upon opening the letter.

2. Failing to accept the offer of a place at Oxford or Cambridge. To attend Oxbridge one must (i) pass the exams, (ii) pass the interview, (iii) accept an offer. Those who fall at this last hurdle qualify for full Reject status the moment that they post their own letter of rejection to an Oxford or Cambridge College.

3. Being sent down from Oxford or Cambridge University before graduating. Those wishing to be considered for mem-

bership under this category must apply to the Department within ten years of leaving. Cases are considered individually on their own merits.

Those who qualify under the first two categories become members of the Society automatically, providing that previously they shall neither have obtained a degree from Oxford or Cambridge, nor have murdered an archbishop. The Membership Department has therefore had little to do in the way of recruitment. Last year, for example, more than thirteen thousand people became members of the Society, despite the fact that all Department staff were on sabbatical leave.

However, the Department will have an increasingly important role to play in the years to come. As the decline in the numbers of young people in this country takes effect, the Society may face a sharp downturn in annual recruitment. Such a demographic trend will force the Department to encourage a higher proportion of school-leavers in each academic year to apply to Oxbridge. If this proves to be insufficient, the Membership Department has contingency plans to encourage the very old and the very young to apply.

To guarantee the continued growth of the Society, the Department encourages people to apply to Oxbridge, whilst working in conjunction with Oxbridge Admissions Tutors to ensure that most of them are rejected. In this latter capacity, the Department is responsible for judging and awarding the prestigious Oxbridge Reject Society Shield. Oxford and Cambridge Admissions Tutors vie annually for this coveted award, which is given to the Tutor responsible for failing the most applicants over the year. First presented last century, the Shield was awarded this year to an Oxford College, bringing Oxford's total of wins to sixty-six. Cambridge has won sixty-nine times and there has been one dead heat.

The Department of Education's Report

The Dean of the Department of Education writes: It is the Society's view that educational standards in this country are rather too high. The Department of Education is therefore fighting a major campaign to lower these standards. At present this is achieved most effectively by encouraging Rejects to become school teachers. The task is an important one, however, and a number of other polcies are also being pursued:

(i) For many years the Department has been encouraging the 'brain-drain'. This has the desirable effects both of reducing the overall intellectual capacity of Great Britain, and of simultaneously increasing the proportion of that intellectual capacity belonging to Rejects. The Department does all in its power to ensure that academics are happy abroad, organizing sherry parties on overseas campuses, and faxing highly complex crossword puzzles to all parts of the world.

(ii) The retention of academic tenure throughout further education (and indeed its introduction into primary and secondary schools) remains one of the Department's cornerstone policies. In this respect we have traditionally had the full support both of the Society (all of whose Departments practise it), and of Britain's academic community.

Much of our effort over the last ten years, however, has had to be directed at the Administrative Supervisor, Ms Alison Clare BA Hons (Oxon) MBA (Harv), who believes that the Society's Departments should remove the right to tenure of post amongst employees. She regards it as 'an outmoded work practice that stifles the introduction of new ideas'. The Department believes that new ideas are rarely an improvement on old ones, and this is therefore precisely the reason that it is fighting to retain tenure.

(iii) Last year the Department began a campaign to encourage the use of random marking in British schools. The Society believes that it is extremely important that young pupils learn that bad work is often mistaken for good work, and that good work does not necessarily bring reward or recognition.

A paper advocating this new policy of random marking was recently published in the *Times Educational Supplement*,

33

and sparked off a fierce debate between readers. Unfortunately we took no part in this subsequent discussion because we do not subscribe to the *T.E.S.* (on principle), so we were unaware that the debate was taking place.

The Department is always searching for new ways to lower British educational standards, and this winter's fact-finding trpi to Bali should be very useful. Bali has been carefully chosen. It is blessed with a higher proportion of illiterate people than Great Britain, performances of *Waiting for Godot* are delightfully rare, and there is a minimal demand for the works of Nietzsche (either in the original German or in Indonesian translation).

The Examinations Department's Report

The Praeceptor of the Board of Reject Studies writes: The Examinations Department prepares and produces examination papers for the Oxford and Cambridge Reject Board of Examinations. The Board has yet to gain full recognition from UCCA, and this, combined with the fact that we maintain a strict policy of marking down, has meant that the Board has yet to be adopted by any school.

Lack of demand for our papers has had some beneficial side effects. It means that we are not required to provide model answers for our examiners, and as a result members of the Department rarely suffer from pre-exam nerves. It also means that 'Examiner for the Oxford and Cambridge Reject Board of Examinations' is one of the least demanding and most sought-after posts in British education.

A Report from the Oxbridge Reject Press

The Editorial Director writes: The Oxbridge Reject Press (ORP) is a small publisher specializing in producing first-edition and remaindered minority-interest books, as well as publishing a number of important works of reference. It is through the ORP that many Rejects first see their work in print.

As one of the first publishers in the country, the ORP has, at one time or another, had dealings with some of the greatest names in English literature. It is now seen as regrettable that William Shakespeare, the playwright, had his plays rejected by the Press because it was felt that the characters were one-dimensional and the plays themselves of little lasting appeal. It is perhaps equally unfortunate that the ORP declined to publish King James' Authorized Version of the Holy Bible, commenting that 'ye language is too moderne and lackyng in ye poetry to be welcomd by any congregation'.

However, the Press has not been entirely without influence in the world of publishing. It was an editor from the ORP, for example, who was to coin the name for a whole category of books: Agatha Christie, the author of detective stories, sent a copy of her first manuscript to the Press, and, after speed-reading it, a rather confused editor admitted in an editorial meeting that it began with a good murder, but that the rest of the book seemed to be about absolutely nothing except 'who done it'. A number of Mrs Christie's books have since been published elsewhere.

The Press can also claim to have published the rarest book in the world. Albert Einstein, the physicist, had published his principle work on relativity elsewhere, but he was persuaded to let the ORP bring out its sequel. Although he had a few reservations about the title suggested by his editor – 'The Return of Relativity' – this was to be the least of the book's problems. At the time the ORP was in the midst of financial difficulties, and the book was typeset extremely badly. There were, on average, forty-three mistakes per page, the majority of them in those sections with more complex formulae. Luckily only the review copies had been sent out by the time that this was discovered, and all but one were swiftly recovered and destroyed. It is believed that the one outstanding copy was stolen by the so-called 'Fifth Man' and smuggled into the Soviet Union. This may well account for the fact that the Soviets have always lagged behind the West in the area of nuclear physics.

Our new publications this year have included *The Oxbridge Reject Dictionary of Misquotations, The Dictionary of Reject Biography* and the first volume of *The Oxbridge Reject Musical Companion to Unfinished Symphonies* (this project has unfortunately run into production difficulties, and work on volumes two and three has had to be halted temporarily).

Ten years after they were first published, the *Oxbridge Reject Study Aids* continue to sell well. These are the only pocket-sized guides currently on the market designed not to aid students revising for their exams, but to help them to come to terms with failing them. A thoroughly revised and updated edition, taking account of recent syllabus changes, is planned for next year.

Other publications soon to appear include:

> *The Fully Illustrated Book of Coffee Tables*
> *Churchill – the Pre-School Years*
> *The Anon and Trad Songbook*
> *Freud on the Interpretation of Dreams (Pop-up Edition)*
> *The Country Diary of an Edwardian Oxbridge Reject*

The Librarian's Report

The Librarian writes: The library was originally established in 1460 to collect all English language first editions. However, by 1481 Caxton had published his fifteenth book (including eight over-sized), and it became clear that stocking a library was going to prove prohibitively expensive. The original policy was consequently abandoned.

The library does still acquire books from time to time, but only if they are either definitive works, capturing the spirit of an age and making an important contribution not only to the literature of the topic but also to the culture of the nation, or if they are written by an Oxbridge Reject.

This year we received the generous donation of eight books. I would like to be able to thank the benefactor, but it appears that they wish to remain anonymus, since the books were left on one of the tables in the library without any indication of whose kindness we should acknowledge. If the donor is reading this report, may I convey our thanks. We did already have the volumes that were donated, but the gift was especially timely as all eight had recently been lost.

One or two of you have complained that our system of cataloguing books is not all it might be. I do know that this is a problem, but I am glad to be able to say that with the installation of the new computer next year, the difficulty of looking up books will be a thing of the past. There is even talk of alphabetical listings by author and subject.

The Statistics Department's Report

The Senior Statistician writes: The Statistics Department was set up twenty years ago to calculate the number of members in the Society.

Although highly accurate mathematical models have now been evolved for the rate at which applicants are rejected by Oxford and Cambridge, the Department has been hampered by the fact that it has little or no data on the rate at which older Rejects are dying. However, recent breakthroughs in numerical analysis based on the supposition that members of the Society are binomially either alive or dead is proving highly exciting.

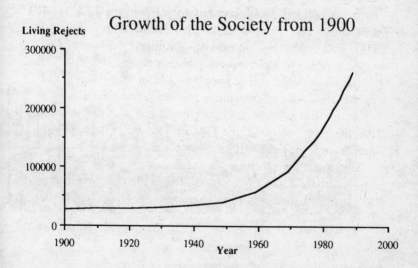

Growth of the Society from 1900

Oxbridge Acceptance and Rejection
1889 - 1989

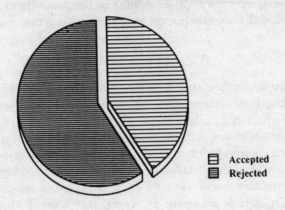

Accepted
Rejected

Oxford & Cambridge Rejects 1974 -1989

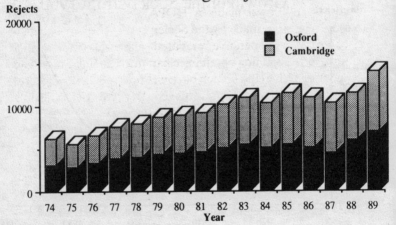

Oxford
Cambridge

A Report from the Department of Photocopying and Data Protection (DOPADAP)

The Controller of Photocopying and Chief Warden of Data writes: This recently merged Department is responsible for all matters appertaining to the provision of photocopying facilities to all Departments within the Society, as well as offering such assistance as may be required in the operation of the said facilities. In addition, DOPADAP ensures that all activities in every Society Department are carried out in full accordance with the strictures laid down in the Data Protection and Copyright Acts. To this end DOPADAP officials regularly scrutinize all lists, memos, letters, postcards, diaries and electronically held data for evidence of any contravention of the said Data Protection and Copyright Acts.

It is anticipated that the part of this undertaking dealing with electronically held data will be subject to a considerable expansion both in duration and magnitude when the Society takes delivery of a computer capable of storing such data.

This year only one infringement of the Copyright Act was recorded, and I am regretful of having to inform that this contravention was made by DOPADAP itself. In response to a submission made by the Society's Light Opera Group, a photocopying operative prepared numerous copies of a libretto without first obtaining clearance from her immediate superior. When the breach of regulations was discovered, all contravening copies were retrieved. DOPADAP is currently considering legal proceedings against itself.

The Legal Department's Report

The Senior Member of the Legal Department writes: The Legal Department (hereinafter and henceforth referred to as 'The Legal Department') was constituted by order of the Governors of the Society with a view to the solution (whether by litigation arbitration negotiation or otherwise howsoever) of disputes and disagreements as to the true and proper construction or interpretation of the statutes ordinances rules regulations and articles of the Society the decision or settlement of issues of a contentious nature arising or occurring between the several departments of the aforesaid and hereinaftermentioned Society and the conduct of any other business of any other nature whatsoever appropriate to the properly constituted functions of the Legal Department WHEREBY sundry actions and proceedings were duly ordered and adjudged (or as the case may be adjudged and ordered) in satisfaction of the claims of the said Society on divers occasions notwithstanding the advice of learned and/or leading counsel that such claims were not maintainable in law or equity and certain other litigation was compromised on terms reasonably satisfactory to the govenors of the aforesaid (but not further hereinaftermentioned) Society.

The Marketing Department's Report

The Director of Marketing writes: we see marketing's functions as twofold: 1. To make Rejects aware of the Society's existence; 2. To assist members of the Society to recognize each other as such.

1. A recent poll has shown that more Rejects than ever before now realize that they are members of the Society. This is the result both of the publicity surrounding the Society's 700th anniversary celebrations, and of the new corporate image commissioned by the Department at a cost of £400,000.

Critics of the new design complain that it is too similar to the old design. This is true. The two designs are indeed identical. This is largely because the extensive market research carried out to choose a new logo was conducted on the Society's existing notepaper. Although not intended for inclusion in the research, our old logo, which was on the notepaper, was chosen by eight out of ten Rejects who expressed a preference.

Members who were not consulted at the time may be interested to judge the rejected designs for themselves.

40

THE
O
X
B
REJECT
SOCIETY
I
D
G
E

The **O**xbridge
R eject
S ociety

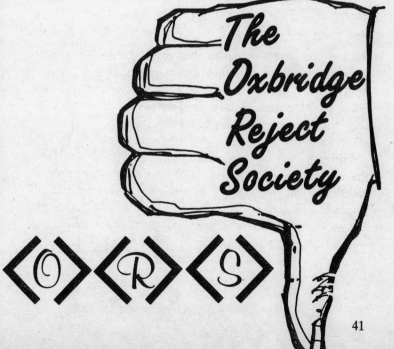

The
Oxbridge
Reject
Society

⟨ O ⟩ ⟨ R ⟩ ⟨ S ⟩

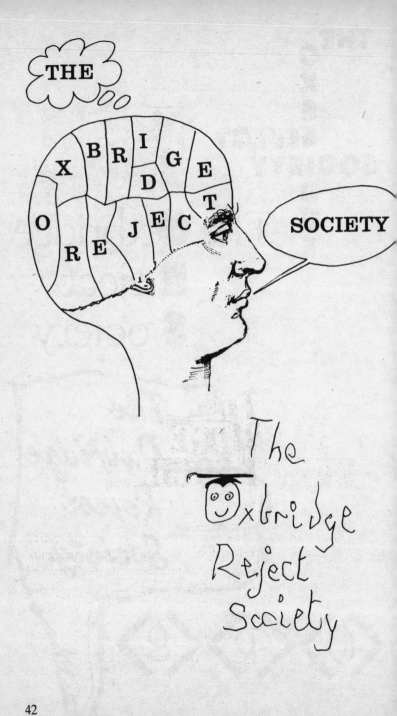

BY DISAPPOINTMENT TO
THE UNIVERSITIES OF
OXFORD AND CAMBRIDGE

THE
OXBRIDGE
REJECT SOCIETY

2. Our research shows that over the last seven hundred years Rejects have found it increasingly difficult to recognize each other. This is clearly an undesirable state of affairs, and the Department has mounted a campaign to remedy the situation. To make identification a little easier the Department has produced the Oxbridge Reject Tie and the Oxbridge Reject Brooch. Designed to be worn at job interviews, both are available from the Society, and members anxious to discover how to obtain them should turn to the postscript at the back of the Prospectus.

The Requisitioning Department's Report

The Head of Requisitioning writes: It has been a good year in Requisitioning. Stocks of extra large paperclips have held up particularly well. Those new yellow wastepaper baskets may have seemed a little bright at first, but I have got used to mine and I am sure that you will grow to like them.

The letter I received notifying me of power cuts this winter now seems to have been a practical joke, and if anyone needs four thousand candles, could they please get in touch.

One complaint though: would people please try not to waste unnecessary quantities of paper. This year we got through about eight and a half times as much Society notepaper as usual, and I don't need to remind you that it doesn't grow on trees.

The Returning Officer's Report

The Returning Officer writes: There have been two elections during the course of the last year. I am pleased to report that, as is usual in Society elections, turnout was low and behaviour was exemplary.

At the suggestion of the Society's Department of the Environment, we use standard *pro forma* voting slips. This removes the need to print ballot papers with individuals' names on them every time that there is an election. Voters simply have to remember whether they are voting for Candidate A, B, C, D or E according to a notice posted at the ballot box. The system has been used in Society elections before and has worked well, but until this Spring we had never had two elections on the same day. I now realize that it was a mistake to use only one ballot box for both elections. However, I feel that under these exceptional circumstances, the compromise that I suggested* was the most sensible.

* *Philip Hatley and Susan Browning (the two Candidates B) were both duly elected to the newly-created positions of Joint-Managers - of - Maintenance - and - Captains - of - Women's - Volleyball.*

44

The Maintenance Department's Report

Philip Hatley writes: I don't know what's been going on whilst I've been off playing volleyball, but this year we've already used eight and a half times more toilet paper than last year, and the Treasurer is beginning to make a fuss.

Otherwise there've been no real problems, but I've had a lot to do, what with the rewiring and decorating to get ready for the new computer – the biggest job I've tackled since the central heating was installed in 1964 – and having to re-paint all those bloody yellow dustbins.

Susan Browning writes: To be honest, I haven't really been a great help to Phil this year, but since April I've had a bit more spare time so I've been helping with some painting.

A Report from the Women in Business Group

The Chairperson writes: This year we have had two more of our very successful Saturday coffee mornings. Very kindly, Lady d'Arling once again made her beautiful Mayfair home available, and the group greatly enjoyed both the lectures held there. Fiona Montagu-Ruttington-Harper talked excitedly on the subject 'Women in Business – Working for an Estate Agent in South-East Belgravia'. There was a lively discussion afterward, and several of those present made use of the opportunity to buy some of the lovely properties highlighted during her talk.

Arabella Nuttington-Crisp spoke very amusingly about 'The Nanny Problem' and brought along a trained English nanny, a sweet Irish girl and a Swedish *au pair* whom she put through a gruelling assessment of their abilities. Each took it in turns to visit Sainsbury's to do a week's shopping for a family of eight (including one diabetic and two vegetarians), and then organize a children's birthday party for 45 three-year-olds, including one who was thought to have recently swallowed a dozen marbles, and another with a suspected cracked skull.

The Fundraising Department's Report

Muriel Botherington writes: This year our loyal team of happy helpers has made a really splendid effort and raised just under £1000, which is a remarkable achievement I'm sure you will agree, so I know you'll all want to join me in saying a big, big thank you to all those who helped out at the Summer Fête and the Sale of Works and who gave so generously of their time and 'know-how'.

Next year we hope to go one better: at my husband Arthur's suggestion we are launching an appeal for £470 million. At one stage we were hoping to raise much of this sum through the sale of the *Mappa Rejecti*. After some initial reluctance, the Society's Senior Archivist finally agreed to sell this ancient map, the work of an Oxbridge Reject cartographer from the Isle of Wight. The Department was able to pursuade the Senior Archivist that the map is neither of any great artistic value, nor of much use as a navigational tool – with Ireland, as it is, off the coast of Norway, and the Isle of Wight double the size of the rest of Britain. Unfortunately, for these very reasons, it has also proved to be worth rather less than we had been expecting.

We are therefore going to rely on tried-and-tested fund raising events such as the Summer Fête, the Raffle and our ever-popular Garden-in-a-Tea-Cup Competition.

The Department of the Environment's Report

The Environment Committee writes: In response to growing anxieties concerning global warming, the Department has instituted a programme of measures to make the Society more 'environmentally friendly'.

Our first campaign has been to encourage the use of recycled paper – which we produce ourselves. Although many Departments have responded well to our appeals for waste paper to recycle, they have failed to supply nearly as much as we need, and to maintain output at full capacity we have had to find some alternative sources. Departments should perhaps be reminded that we can use any sort of paper in our recycling mill, be it writing paper, loo paper or even crumbling old documents. The Department is pleased to announce that production of recycled paper is presently 850% higher than at the same period last year.

The Department is also responsible for monitoring evidence of the 'Greenhouse' effect, and has been busy analysing the data provided over the last century by our Meteorological Unit. One of the principal, and most disturbing findings of the study was the identification of a notable increase in the temperature of the Society's offices since 1964. It has recently been pointed out, however, that this may be less the result of any global trend, and more the consequence of the installation of central heating in that year.

The Genetic Engineering Department's Report

The Genetic Engineer writes: The Genetic Engineering Department is attempting to trace the degree to which failing Oxbridge may be hereditary. The Department is trying to isolate the dominant Reject gene, but is hampered to some extent by clauses in the Society Constitution banning experiments on living Rejects.

As a result of this limitation, the Department decided some years ago to conduct all of its research using chimpanzees. To achieve the highest possible levels of accuracy it was decided that, before any experiments began, the chimpanzees should fail Oxbridge.

After a little coaching by the Department, one chimp applied last year, and two this year. All three got in. The experiment was thus deemed to have failed, and was abandoned last month. All three chimpanzees have now been withdrawn from their undergraduate or postgraduate studies and, happily, have been found employment within the Society. One is working here in the Genetic Engineering Department, and two have jobs in the post-room.

The Post Room's Report

The Administrative Supervisor writes: I have yet to receive the post room's report, although – as far as I can understand – they claim to have sent it last week. I'm surprised, because every time I've passed the Post Room recently I've heard frenzied typing, but all I've received from them so far is a great deal of typed gibberish, two sonnets and the first act of Hamlet.

The Reject Fine Art Commission's Report

The Director of the Commission writes: I have been able to spend little time with the Commission during the course of the year, owing to my duties as Senior Archivist to the Society.

For those who do not know, the Commission advises on all matters regarding the interpretation of the aesthetic, whether in art or architecture. To this end it has made several recommendations to relevant Departments during the course of the year.

The Commission advised on the decoration of the new computer room, carried out between February and July this year. A traditional colour scheme of gold and 'Adam' green regency-stripe wallpaper, with the ceiling relieved in white on a 'Wedgewood' blue base, and a crimson carpet was finally agreed upon, thereby creating a dynamic tension between the modernity of the technology and the tradition embodied in the longevity of the Society, expressed in a neo-classical idiom. Unfortunately much of this scheme had to be abandoned when the room was subsequently rewired, sound-proofed and air-conditioned, and the carpet removed to prevent the build-up of static.

The Commission was also involved in the development of plans for the proposed extension to the Society's Archive, housing surplus papers and allowing the public display of visual material contained within the collection. In consultation with the Senior Archivist, the Commission prepared a detailed brief for two leading firms of architects. This stated that the planned extension should be designed to resemble a monstrous carbuncle on the face of a much-loved and elegant friend.

The first response proposed that a large glass pyramid be constructed in the car-park. This was rejected on the grounds that it was too much in harmony with the existing building, created no visual interest, and would make parking very difficult. The second response, which was accepted, proposed a highly original and exciting extension which offered a unique solution to the constraints of space and budget available. Controversially, all wiring, plumbing and air-conditioning was hidden on the inside, with all functional areas, rooms and staircases on the outside. It was felt that the planned construction would create a sense of space, integrate with the natural surroundings, and provide highly open-plan offices, with plenty of room for parking. Although some anxieties were expressed that the total absence of outside walls would make the building draughty, the Commission was fully reassured on this point by the architects, who argued that it was of paramount importance to begin construction as soon as possible, since the designs had already won a dozen major awards, including two from the RIBA.

The Society Archives' Report

The Senior Archivist writes: I have been able to spend little time in the Archive during the course of the year, owing to my duties as Director of the Reject Fine Art Commission. However I can report that plans for a new wing to be added to the Archive have been dropped following a recent reorganization of our collection. It seems that last year's calculations were completely wrong, and that we do in fact have eight-and-a-half times less material than we originally suspected.

The Space Programme's Report

The Chief Scientist writes: The Oxbridge Reject Space Agency was established by Henry Milne, Chairman of Governors from 1961–63, who pledged that the Society would send a Reject into space before an Oxbridge Graduate got there. The Society was at the time suffering from a crisis of confidence, and Milne's pledge, although correctly interpreted as a wildly over-ambitious publicity stunt, caught the imagination of Rejects everywhere.

Although little was achieved under Milne's leadership, still less has been done under that of his successors. Society Treasurers have recognized that the Society cannot afford to spend money on space exploration, and the Department, from its inception, has remained the smallest and least funded in the Society.

What the Space Programme lacks in resources it makes up for in determination. But while it has never been short of ideas, few have got further than the drawing board. Sadly, funding problems and cut-backs in supplies of chalk now mean that, in future, many may not even make it that far.

Despite its enthusiasm, the Agency's successes have not been numerous. Initial experimental launches had to be abandoned when no pet animal could be found to volunteer for the mission, and the Space Programme has been dogged with such setbacks ever since.

During the subsequent delays it was decided to abandon plans for a simple orbiting flight and join the race to put a man on the moon. It is now generally accepted by the Society (and the three Rejects selected for the mission) that it was fortunate that this race was lost. Our scientists had failed to take into account either the fact that the earth is rotating, or that the moon has no atmosphere. This latter detail might have rendered our moon buggy – a second-hand MG Convertible – a little impractical.

Undeterred, and despite the fact that costs in this sector are rocketing, the Programme is now planning to construct a space probe. Although a launch date has yet to be set, some details have already been worked out. There are plans for the satellite to pass Mars, before continuing its marathon journey further into the galaxy of the Milky Way. The probe will emit a message of goodwill that has already been recorded by our Chairman of Governors, Arthur Botheringв ton, and includes, at his own suggestion, his memorable rendition of 'My Way'. It is hoped that the probe, REJECT

I, will encourage fairly advanced life forms to make contact with the Society. It was to have carried a small transmitter for this purpose, but unless funding is increased substantially in the near future, it now seems likely that any extra-terrestrials will have to make use of a small supply of stamped, self-addressed envelopes.

The Central Policy Review Committee's Report

The Administrative Supervisor writes: there seems to be some doubt as to the purpose of the newly-formed Central Policy Review Committee, or – as some seem to delight in calling it – the 'Think Tank'. I am writing here to dispel, once and for all, the idea that this organisation is anything other than a forum for the putting forward and discussion of radical and mould-breaking ideas, and the examination of feasible modes of implementation for such ideas. Although there are no actual Oxbridge Rejects on the Committee, I felt it appropriate to include our own report here, to demonstrate that the considerable running expenses incurred are more than adequately justified, and to quell any rumours of 'plots' or 'conspiracies'. There is certainly no mystery involved.

Unfortunately we are not ready to talk about some of the ideas put forward at the Committee, but I can assure you that all Departments will receive full instructions in due course. However, the schemes that we are intending to put into practice over the period to 1 April, include:

– a system of unscheduled and unannounced departmental assessments, with, in each case, the next year's budget to be based on measured performance. To be conducted by a newly-formed Independent Review Body to be chaired by myself in my capacity as Administrative Supervisor.

– a cost-apportioning scheme for internal accounting pur-poses, whereby individual Departments invoice each other for services provided. This will introduce some much-needed financial realism into the Society, and will allow proper budgeting. This scheme to be operated through a newly-created Audit Office, separate from the Treasury, and chaired by myself in my capacity as Administrative Supervisor.

– a programme of reassessment for work practices within all Departments, with particular reference to tenure, sabbatical 'leave' and fact-finding 'missions'. To be conducted by a newly-formed Contracts Department, to be largely autonomous, but to be chaired by myself in my capacity as Administrative Supervisor.

– a broad-based study to examine opportunities for reducing the Society's complex bureaucratic structure and limiting the number of Departments. A new Department to be set up to achieve a fifty per cent reduction in departmental numbers over two years, and to be chaired by myself in my capacity as Administrative Supervisor.

The Annual Accounts

A Financial Summary by Murray Buesst,
*Treasurer, Secretary of the Chest and Chief
Accountant, The Oxbridge Reject Society*

If I am to sum up the Oxbridge Reject Society's last financial year in one word it must be 'steady progress'.

During my two years in office, the Treasury has undergone a radical change of direction, and I am glad to be able to report that much of the good work which I announced last year is now beginning to bear fruit: our asset base has been cut back significantly, investment is at a record low and overall borrowing has been approximately doubled. Nevertheless, there is a great deal still to be achieved if we are to regain the relatively comfortable financial position which the Society enjoyed during the 1540s and 50s.

It would not be appropriate here to examine the individual contributions made by successive Treasurers to the steady decline since those golden years. Indeed to do so would be extremely difficult, since for the most part there is no record of their names. All the indications are, however, that I am the very first Treasurer of the Oxbridge Reject Society to have trained in accountancy. Were it not for the fact that nobody told me there might be questions on Agricultural Partial Averaging in my PE1 Tax exam, I would also be the first Treasurer of the Oxbridge Reject Society to have qualified.

Many of you will have read my contribution to last year's annual report, 'Why the Treasury Needs a Very Big Computer', and I am glad to be able to announce to you this year that all its recommendations have been accepted and are in the process of being implemented. I have no doubt that the installation of the new mainframe (with its facilities for single tasking, batch-processing, half-duplex communication, limited RAM and state-of-the-art IBM incompatibility) will prove beneficial to all areas of the Society's work.

One of the principal tasks of the last year has been to regularize all of the Society's accounts in preparation for their transfer onto the new computer. This has proved an expensive and time-consuming undertaking and some people have actually questioned the need to have computerized accounts stretching as far back as 1290. To these critics I would answer that if sound financial management is to be achieved then it is essential that the fullest picture be presented, and to that end it has been a most valuable exercise. Indeed there have already been two very significant benefits. First, I have been able to sort out all irregularities in the Society's accounts – from the failure of past Treasurers to include a valuation of the goodwill engendered by the Society's brand name, to establishing that the Society had an outstanding window tax liability for the period 1735–41. Secondly, it has enabled me to compile, at our Chairman of Governors' request, the extended report which follows, entitled 'The Treasury from its Founding to the Present Day'.

The last year has been an exciting time for the Treasury. We have continued to push the boundaries of modern finance a little further forward, and our approach remains as radical and innovative as ever. In July, for example, the Oxbridge Reject Society introduced the world's financial markets to the Off-shore eX-coupon Bullet Redeemable Inti Denominated Geared Evergreen Retractable Extendable Junior Euro-Convertible Traded (OXBRIDGEREJECT) bond.

Our pioneering approach is not the only thing that has attracted attention over the last year, however, and many of the Society's members will have been aware of the active role that I played in a recent insider dealing investigation conducted by the Serious Fraud Office. This is just one of the responsibilities which the post of Treasurer entails, and it was both a duty and a pleasure to offer the police – on behalf of the Society – what assistance I could with their enquiries.

Nonetheless, my arrest and subsequent prosecution was a traumatic time, and I would like to take this opportunity to thank all those who stood by me throughout, particularly the

54

redoubtable Ernest Thring, Senior Member of the Society's Legal Department. Few lawyers, surely, would have thought to have defended their client's innocence – and secured his freedom – in such an ingenious way. It is a tribute to his skill that the judge ruled, on appeal, that 'only the *profitable* use of inside information can constitute a criminal act'.

I am often asked why it is necessary for the Society to have funds of its own. There are three answers: first, of course, if the Society had no funds, there would be nothing for the Treasurer to do; secondly, the Society supports a considerable bureaucracy comprising a large number of Departments, all requiring financial support; thirdly, the Society is, by its very nature, dependent upon the Universities of Oxford and Cambridge. Consequently it is, as the Membership Secretary is fond of reminding me, essential that these fine Universities continue to attract large numbers of student applications, whilst maintaining such high standards that the majority must be rejected. This is a very expensive business, so for hundreds of years the Society has been happy to offer financial assistance to both Oxford and Cambridge, thereby ensuring itself an ever increasing annual intake of new members.

Regrettably the Society's own financial situation has not been at all healthy for the last few years, and following an unexpectedly large demand from the Inland Revenue for prompt settlement of an inflation-adjusted, outstanding window tax liability, donations to Oxford and Cambridge have recently had to be stopped. I appreciate the hardship that this causes, and sincerely hope that payments can be resumed before any real damage is done to academic standards.

This concludes my report on the last financial year. Unfortunately full accounts are not yet available for publication, since the auditors claim to have found some 'irregularities of accounting methods' – evidence, no doubt, of their poor training and insufficient understanding of the most up-to-date practices. It has therefore only been possible to provide an Income and Expenditure Account (including Exceptional and Extraordinary Items, but without a detailed breakdown of Departmental administration expenses).

It was, I think, the eminent economist, poet and town-planner, John Milton Keynes – a man for whom I have the greatest admiration – who said 'Let bygones be bygones'. It is in this spirit that I now present my septecentenary report.

Murray Buesst,
*Treasurer, Secretary of the Chest
and Chief Accountant,
The Oxbridge Reject Society*

The Treasury
from its Founding to the Present Day

The Asset Management Division

In its earliest years the Society received most of its assets from bequests. These were made in the wills of Rejects, many of whom had been born into positions of considerable wealth. As a result, within a century or so of its founding, the Society had become one of the largest land owners in the country and held substantial reserves of gold.

In addition, by around 1400 it had acquired a quite remarkable portfolio of rights and privileges. Accounts dating from 1417 record, for example, that the Society not only maintained, under Royal Warrant, a monopoly on the importation of French mineral water, but that it also possessed mining rights over a large area of what had been Mercia (as well as much of the North Sea), and held a most lucrative franchise, granted by Pope Boniface IX, to sell Holy Relics in Cornwall.

Sadly, successive generations of early Rejects proved particularly adept at squandering vast sums, and although right up to the present day Rejects have been commendably loyal in remembering the Society in their wills, they have rarely been in a position to match the generosity of the Society's early members.

Falling income from bequests put considerable pressure on the Society's finances, and as gold reserves steadily declined, successive Treasurers were forced to look for alternative sources of revenue. Detailed accounts from 1488 record a comprehensive rationalization of the Society's assets. The French mineral water rights, which had proved to be a source of negligible income, were sold for twelve shillings, and the Mercian mining entitlements were allowed to revert to the Crown, thereby saving the Society a further four pence *per annum*. The Cornish Relic franchise was retained, and indeed has been held by the Society to this day.

The Venture Capital Division

In an attempt to return the Society to the prosperity of its earliest years, the Treasury made the decision to diversify into a number of financial markets – including that of venture capital. It was during the 1488 financial rationalization that the Venture Capital Division was set up, and this has been hailed by some as the most significant financial advance that the Society has ever made.

Such a view is based largely on the fact that the Venture Capital Division is the only section of the Treasury that has consistently met financial targets. Although this is undoubtedly true, my own view is that these targets have simply been set too low. Consequently I believe that the Division has not come even close to fulfilling its objective. The Venture Capital Division has, in point of fact, made no investments of any kind since it was first set up.

Such a disappointing performance cannot be explained by any shortage of investment opportunities. For most of the fifteenth century the Division was the only independent financial institution offering today's equivalent of risk capital; yet it completely failed to exploit its dominance of the market. Recently discovered copies of correspondence with Christopher Columbus confirm this point.

The Division was first approached in 1490 by Columbus, who sought financial backing for a voyage in search of a new route to the Orient. The Division wrote thanking him for his interest, stating that his letter was receiving their attention. Two months later they wrote again, asking for a detailed business plan, a *curriculum vitae* and the names and addresses of two referees. On receipt of these documents, a further correspondence ensued, in which it was suggested that Columbus's estimates for barrels of salt beef were perhaps 'a little unrealisticke', bearing in mind the harsh winter; and was he aware that 'Pethericke's, Chandlers of Truro, at presente be offeringe to corke ye hulle and lower decke of two shippes for ye pryce o' one?'.

A fifth letter enquired about the proposed equity split, and asked Columbus what security he was intending to offer the Society. Following this, a detailed survey was carried out on his principle place of residence which noted 'ye possibilitie of isolated outbreakes of dry rot in concealed load-bearing tymbers which it has not beene possible to inspecte, and a poor state of decorative repair throughout, requiryng some considrable worke.'

In 1491 the Treasurer finally called a meeting with the managers of the Venture Capital Division to settle the matter. The minutes note that after a brief discussion the Senior Manager put forward the view of his Division that Columbus should not be offered Society funds, explaining that Columbus 'has no proven tracke record of discoveryng either new trade routes or continents of untolde wealth'. The Treasurer expressed his great relief at this decision, as he had believed it would be morally reprehensible for the Society to encourage anyone to sail off the edge of the world.

The Division's four-word contribution to the Annual Report of 1491 was picked up widely by the financial press at the time, and the phrase 'Nothing ventured, nothing gained' has been much quoted since. The Division's policy has, regrettably, changed little since this period. Indeed, it was only through my intervention since taking office that those funds which it did have at its disposal were placed in an interest-bearing bank account, previous Division Managers having regarded this as 'far too risky'.

The Division for the Depositing of Monies

Although at one time the most profitable of all the Treasury's activities, the Society was only briefly involved with the receiving of money to be held on deposit. The Division was set up by Philip de Bon Coeur, Society Treasurer during much of the reign of Henry VIII. Following the fall from grace of Cardinal Wolsey, de Bon Coeur became one of Henry's most trusted advisors, and it was he who was chosen to oversee the financial aspects of the Dissolution of the Monasteries.

It may be supposed that de Bon Coeur was secretly sympathetic to the plight of the monasteries, for much of the money raised through the sale of monastic valuables and land was channelled through the Society's Treasury, and remained there. de Bon Coeur was doubtless biding his time, and waiting for a suitable moment to return to the monks what was rightfully theirs. However we shall never know for certain, because soon after the deposits were made, de Bon Coeur drowned after suffering a surfeit of lampreys and collapsing into a butt of malmsey wine.

No other member of the Treasury had been aware of the vast sums being held for the monasteries, and because de Bon Coeur had, shortly before his death, destroyed all financial records by cutting them into very thin strips, it was not until some years later that the source of the money was discovered. By then most of the monasteries had vanished altogether, and, in any case, the accounting paperwork involved in returning the deposits would have taken weeks. The £173,249 18s. 6d. windfall did much to improve the Society's finances, and indeed its effects are still enjoyed today.

The Commercial Property Division

In the mid-sixteenth century the Society's Commercial Property Division was established to manage the Society's property interests. At the time, its portfolio was considerable, but after an extended period of contraction only one important set of assets now remains, namely the freehold to the land on which fourteen Oxford and Cambridge Colleges currently stand.

Under the terms of the leases the annual rents have remained fixed (at fourteen pence each) and are now somewhat below market rates. Indeed, in consideration of the sums involved and because of the special relationship which it enjoys with both Universities, the Society has not sought to collect any rent from Oxford or Cambridge for over three hundred years. But financial difficulties of our own mean that this situation will have to change when the leases come up for renewal in 1997.

The Division regrets that these negotiations may be hampered by the fact that the relevant title documents have not been seen by the Society Archivist or the Legal Department since the last Society Inventory in 1665.

The Mining Division

The seventeenth and eighteenth centuries were, above all else, 'Centuries of Discovery'. The Oxbridge Reject Society was determined not to miss out, and in 1834 the Reject Geographical Society was established. In its first decade it discovered many things, although nothing entirely new, but its moment of glory came in 1845, when a Reject Expedition found gold in the foothills outside San Francisco. The goldrush that followed was one of the largest ever seen. It was also the shortest. The expedition had in fact discovered nothing more than pyrite, or, as it is still known in the area, Reject's Gold.

At the height of the excitement over the expedition's discovery, the Treasury set up the Mining Division. When the truth about the San Francisco find was revealed, the new Division began to look elsewhere for mining interests. It made considerable real estate investments in Australia, acquiring a number of smallholdings in Northern Victoria and a very sizeable estate in Queensland. Both areas were claimed by the vendors to be rich in gold. This was indeed discovered to be the case in Northern Victoria, and the Society would have made a considerable sum but for the dishonesty of the managing agent employed there. The Queensland estate did not yield any precious metals and was subsequently sold at a reasonable profit to the Kookaburra Mining Corporation – now one of the world's largest suppliers of uranium.

The Division of Agriculture and Fisheries

Large parts of Africa were colonized by Europeans during the nineteenth century. This offered an opportunity which the Division of Agriculture and Fisheries was keen to exploit. An extensive acreage of land was purchased for the cultivation of pistachio nuts, but sadly the Division was not provided with the additional resources to despatch Oxbridge Rejects to manage these estates, and it was further hampered by the slow and unreliable communications of the day. As a result, several years had elapsed before the unusually intensive farming being practised by many of the tenants came to light, and the Pistachio Nut Scheme was halted. By this time most of the Society's estates in the Northern Sahara had become notably less productive.

The Society's fishing rights have also not been a source of revenue for some years. During its principal purchase of fishing waters off the coast of Holland in 1713, the Legal Department understandably failed to notice a tiny clause in the Treatry of Utrecht specifying that it was the coastline depicted on a map by Johannes Berg dating from 1474 to which the Society held rights. As the Dutch have worked extensively on moving their coastline westwards since this date, the Society has been left with the fishing rights to a large area of arable farmland.

The Shipping Division

In order to exploit the Society's worldwide interests, the Treasury invested heavily in shipping during the nineteenth century. For several decades it operated a highly profitable fleet of clippers, but towards the end of the century suffered a series of losses at sea. These, coupled with the advent of steam, proved disastrous for the Shipping Division and by the 12 April, 1912, its once proud fleet had been reduced to just one ship. Stock-taking by the Treasurer the following week revealed that this too had been lost.

When the news of the sinking of the Titanic first reached the Society, the Head of Shipping vividly captured the feeling in his Division's offices when he noted in the ledger that it was 'very quiet indeed'. This was not primarily a result of the fact that the Titanic had been built with revolutionary 'All-Weather Plating' designed by a Reject, but because the Society owned a considerable stake in the ship – which it had been due to float on the stock market the following week.

Following the sinking, the Head of the Division spent a hectic week telephoning members to assure them that the vessel had indeed been fully insured. As a result it was a further fortnight before he realized that the policy had been taken out with the Society's own insurance syndicate.

The Stockbroking Division

It was the Titanic experience, more than any other, that convinced the Society that it should, in future, invest in smaller projects and do so through the purchase of stocks and shares. On the advice of the Economic Research Division, much of this investment took place on Wall Street. The Society's investments performed well for a number of years, and it was only a small misunderstanding that converted these significant gains into equally significant losses.

Owing, no doubt, to a lack of proper training, the Senior Member of the Stockbroking Division had failed to master the current financial jargon. When told in 1919 that the Society would be well advised to make its assets more 'liquid', he sold the Society's entire portfolio and bought four distilleries, twenty-three vineyards and a chain of bars stretching right across the United States. Profits were not increased by the introduction of prohibition the followng year.

The Commodity Broking Division

After a brief period of dealing on the futures exchanges of the world, the Society has withdrawn from active involvement in commodity broking. In the Treasury it is now widely accepted that contracts in commodities such as coffee or tin should be sold before they expire – otherwise the products are delivered when the contract matures. However, the Head of the Division had previously only worked in our Maintenance Department. He set out to build up a portfolio of interests, a number of which matured before he sold them. This in itself would not have been a serious problem, had the first three contracts not been for oil, potassium nitrate and sugar. These were delivered simultaneously and the whole of the Commodity Broking Division was killed in the subsequent explosion.

The Mergers and Acquisitions Division

In the early 1970s the Treasurer conducted a feasibility study to assess the viability of a Society Bank, which could both be profitable and offer a useful service to Rejects. The report was encouraging, and in anticipation of establishing the service, the Treasury set about obtaining a Mergers and Acquisitions Division. The Acquisitions team was acquired by the Treasury from a highly respected American merchant bank in 1975. In 1978 it was merged with the newly formed Mergers Division. Ernest Thring of the Legal Department was responsible for uniting the two, since at this time the Mergers arm had had no experience of merging anything quite as large as itself.

To facilitate a swift integration of these two Divisions, Ernest Thring made the recommendation that 'the Manager of Mergers, formerly Senior Manager of Venture Capital, become Joint Deputy Chairman of the combined Department answering to the Treasurer who should sit as Chairman of the Board while the Chairman of Acquisitions should be made Joint Deputy Chairman together with the Manager of the Mergers arm but without executive power.' This suggestion was finally abandoned because of problems with implementation.

Having had Thring's proposals rejected, the Legal Department refused to do any further work, and the Division had to adopt as simple a structure as possible. Mergers and Acquisitions therefore became a co-operative, with members of the Division taking it in turns to make executive decisions.

This had not previously been a problem, but this year the Division bought two companies: the Isle of Lewis Fishing and Whaling Company and a well-known American hamburger chain. It now appears that these purchases were the result of some confusion about the terms 'net' and 'gross' profit. The man responsible for these deals, Mr Hamish McCloud, has been moved to a position more suited to his abilities.

Plans to establish the Oxbridge Reject Bank were abandoned in 1980. The Mergers and Acquisitions Division is currently engaged in secret negotiations with itself, and it is believed that these may result in a management buy-out.

The Economic Research Division

The Society's Economic Research Division has enjoyed a history of considerable success. I am delighted to be able to report that it anticipated the South Sea Company catastrophe well in advance, as well as the stock market crashes of 1929 and 1987. It accurately predicted the growth of the canal system in the United Kingdom and the subsequent predominance of the railways that rapidly made canals uncompetitive. It even foresaw the enormous demand for the Rubik Cube, those sticky yellow memo pads and the plastic Japanese flowers that dance to music. It is a great pity that the Division never thought it necessary to pass on any of these forecasts.

CONCLUSION

Although the Society has yet to regain the levels of prosperity enjoyed in the fifteenth and sixteenth centuries, we continue to strive towards this goal. One learns from one's mistakes, and indeed much has been learned over the last seven hundred years.

It would be foolish to expect too much of the new computer, but I am convinced that it will transform work practices, improve efficiency enormously and revolutionize hand-to-eye co-ordination throughout the Society. It will also be the stepping stone that will allow us to return to financial stability and growth after a rather extended absence. I look forward to being able to write, in next year's report, that the computer's installation has gone very smoothly and that it is rapidly justifying the considerable research and development costs already incurred.

Treasurer's Addendum
Since the time of writing the above report, I have been advised that a new generation of information technology will soon become available that might render the proposed computer obsolete. Clearly I would not like to be responsible for the purchase of a 'white elephant', and consequently plans for the computer's installation have been postponed whilst a report into the advantages of this new generation is prepared.

The Accounts of the Oxbridge Reject Society

The Annual Audit has yet to be concluded. The Income & Expenditure Account is detailed below, but a full breakdown of Departmental administration expenses is currently being reviewed by the auditors, and I will be sending them the balance sheet the moment that I can get it to balance.

I must, however, take this opportunity to warn members that the growth forecasts that I made last year now seem to be a little optimistic, and that our analysts appear to have been correct when they recently downgraded them.

INCOME AND EXPENDITURE ACCOUNT	Notes	YEAR ENDED 1 APRIL	
		Current year £	Prior year £
Income:			
Bequests		867,739	525,205
Local government grants		22,450	20,987
Interest receivable and similar income	2	31,418,512	27,937,616
Other income	3	255,652	198,008
		32,564,353	28,681,816
Expenditure:			
Payments to Universities	4	—	(20,907,434)
Travel Fund expenditure		(3,566)	(271)
Administration expenses		(4,543,886)	(4,532,659)
Exceptional items	5	(1,042,907)	(29,758)
Net income from ordinary activities		26,973,994	3,211,694
Extraordinary items	6	(26,974,002)	(254)
Net income for the financial year		(£8)	£3,211,440

NOTES TO THE INCOME AND EXPENDITURE ACCOUNT

1 Accounting policies

These accounts have been prepared on an historic cost basis and in accordance with generally accepted accounting practice, including the Accounting Standards Committee exposure draft ED38 'Accounting by Charities', except in cases for which such practice would be inconvenient.

2 Interest receivable and similar income

	Current year £	Prior year £
Interest from monies held upon deposit	31,351,094	27,886,229
Interest from Venture Capital current account	10,458	–
Inland Revenue (Charitable Status Rebate)	56,960	51,387
	£31,418,512	£27,937,616

3 Other income

	Current year £	Prior year £
Net income from the Oxbridge Reject Press	254,760	197,996
Summer Fête	892	12
Sale of Holy Relics (Cornwall)	–	–
	£255,652	£198,008

4 Payments to Universities

	Current year £	Prior year £
Payments to Cambridge University	–	10,453,717
Payments to Oxford University	–	10,453,717
	–	£20,907,434

5 Exceptional items

	Current year £	Prior year £
Design fees (Marketing Department)	400,000	–
Historical Research Department	126,907	23,778
Central Policy Review Committee	498,000	–
Computer Research costs	18,000	5,980
	£1,042,907	£29,758

6 Extraordinary items

	Current year £	Prior year £
Adjustment for prior year Inland Revenue Window Tax liability (1735–41)	(5)	–
Interest charged upon overdue taxation (effective rate of 6.25%)	(25,873,148)	–
	(25,873,153)	–
Third World debt rescheduling	(349)	(254)
Loss incurred through launch of Off-shore eX-coupon Bullet Redeemable Inti Denominated Geared Evergreen Retractable Extendable Junior Euro-Convertible Traded bonds	(1,100,500)	–
	(£26,974,002)	(254)

Society News

The Annual General Meeting

The AGM was, as usual, held at 23a Edwardes Square, London W8, at 7pm on 1 April.

1. Apologies for Absence: the Membership Secretary apologized for being unable to name those who were absent.

2. Minutes of the Last Meeting: the Secretary to the Governors read out the minutes of the previous year's AGM. The Chairman then called upon the meeting to ratify these minutes.

At this point the Senior Member of the Legal Department pointed out that the minutes of the last AGM could not be ratified because, according to the minutes, the meeting had not been quorate. He further noted that the Constitution specified a quoracy level of one tenth of the total membership. He also observed that this had not been achieved since 1291.

The Chairman of Governors then asked the Senior Member of the Legal Department what steps should be taken to lower the quoracy levels specified in the Constitution, in order that minutes might, in future, be ratified, and resolutions passed.

The Senior Member replied that the answer given in previous years remained applicable: that this would require a constitutional amendment which, constitutionally, could only be passed by a majority vote taken at a quorate Annual General Meeting.

The Chairman called upon the Membership Secretary to make a count of members present at the meeting to establish whether quoracy had been achieved.

While this count was in progress, Dr Olivia Pegge of the Statistics Department announced that there were now estimated to be 252,160 members of the Society.

The result of the count was then announced. All present agreed that the Membership Secretary had not miscounted, and that there were indeed fewer than 25,216 Rejects present.

3. Any Other Business: it was resolved (unanimously) that the meeting be concluded, but that, at the invitation of the landlord, all present remain on the premises until closing time. This decision was not ratified.

Note to members from the Secretary to the Governors: whilst these minutes are intended to provide a true and correct record of the proceedings of the 700th Annual General Meeting of the Oxbridge Reject Society, they are still subject to ratification at next year's AGM.

An Interview with the Retiring Chairman of Governors

As many members will be aware, the Chairman of Governors, Mr Arthur Botherington, is retiring shortly. Here his close friend and successor, Mr Hamish McCloud, talks to the Chairman at his country home. What follows is an edited selection of some of the topics discussed.

Hamish McCloud: 'Well it is delightful, Chairman, to be here with you in front of a blazing fire; and may I say that this fruit cake is particularly good.'

Arthur Botherington: 'Oh, I'm so glad you like it. My wife Muriel makes it. Actually I can't eat it myself, you know, on account of . . . well, you know.'

Hamish McCloud: 'Now, tell me, Chairman, why have you decided to stand down as Chairman of Governors?'

Arthur Botherington: 'Well none of us is getting any younger, and I suppose that it was inevitable that the time should come when I felt it was right to make way for some new blood. Of course, I am proud to have been Chairman during this most historic year, but now I feel it is time to let another Reject run the straight race.'

Hamish McCloud: 'Well I'll certainly do my best. As you say, Chairman, this is the Society's 700th Anniversary.

70

Do you feel it has changed much over this period?'

Arthur Botherington: 'Oh, yes; after all, we have seen changes over the last seven centuries which have touched almost every aspect of our lives. Naturally, the Society has moved with the times, and no doubt the founder members would scarcely recognize the Society today. But nonetheless it is something of a tribute to Rejects over the years that, despite the passage of time, the Society has retained, undiminished, all of its founding ideals.'

Hamish McCloud: 'What exactly *are* these founding ideals?'

Arthur Botherington: 'Dear me. That is a good question, and to be perfectly frank, the Secretary is rather more of an expert on this than I am. But I do know that they are definitely undiminished.'

Hamish McCloud: 'Can you point to any specific changes since 1290?'

Arthur Botherington: 'Well, the Society is now significantly older than it was then.'

Hamish McCloud: 'Wise words, indeed, Chairman; thank you. You have been Chairman of Governors for almost four years. What do you feel that your main contribution has been over this period?'

Arthur Botherington: 'Well, to be honest I have always seen the role of Chairman as a one of support and encouragement rather than direct intervention or specific action. Not for me, thank you Muriel – more tea for you, Hamish? I mean, the last thing you want is someone who gets it into their head to play an active role; that can be very disruptive.

'But while I have been Chairman I do know that much has been achieved, and although I have not been able to attend very many meetings over the past four years, I understand that there are many more things in the pipeline to which lots of members are looking forward.'

Hamish McCloud: 'But surely you wouldn't want to claim that as Chairman you had made no specific contributions to the Society?'

Arthur Botherington: 'No, I wouldn't say that at all – sugar?

As Chairman of Governors I believe I have had my share of successes over the years. Muriel often reminds me that I have also had my share of failures, but I like to think that my efforts have not been in vain, and that as I have watched the Society grow a little older, it may also have become a little wiser.'

Hamish McCloud: 'Have you any regrets, Chairman?'

Arthur Botherington: 'Regrets? I've had few. But then again, too few to mention.'

Hamish McCloud: 'And what of your future plans?'

Arthur Botherington: 'Well, Muriel and I are looking forward to a well-earned retirement here in the country, and we trust that all of our friends in the Society will come and visit whenever they are passing.'

Hamish McCloud: 'Well I've no doubt of that. Lastly, Chairman, I would like to ask a question which I know that many other members sometimes ask themselves: How do you think that your life might have differed had you been accepted by those Oxbridge Admissions Tutors?'

Arthur Botherington: 'I suppose that one answer must be that, but for my rejection, I would not be sitting here with you, Hamish, for I could never have been elected to the auspicious post of Chairman of Governors of the Oxbridge Reject Society, a development which I consider to have been the crowning point of my career. Then again, I would not have met Muriel, who has played such an important part in my life. When one considers these things I think one must surely conclude with Robert Frost that:

> Two roads diverged in a wood, and I –
> I took the one less travelled by,
> And that has made all the difference.'

A full recording of this interview has been stored in the Society Archive and placed under a seventy-three year restriction order.

Lectures

Next year's Reject Lecture will be held on 21 March at the Guildhall. The Reverend William Peterson will deliver an address entitled: 'Could God pass Oxbridge?' There will be no discussion afterwards.

Early in the New Year, the Society's Treasurer, M. W. Buesst Esq., will be giving three short introductory talks entitled: 'You and the New Computer'.

At 9 am every Monday morning of this year, Ms Alison Clare BA Hons (Oxon) MBA (Harv), the Society's Administrative Supervisor, will be lecturing on 'Pursuing Expansionary Pro-active Strategies Through Hierarchical Restructuring'. Ms Clare's lectures will not be held in the Smythson Hall, as they were last year, but in the smaller Squirrel Room. There will be a £4 admission charge (OAPs and UB40s: £4).

Reject News and Notices

Members are reminded that motions for the Society's next AGM should be sent to the Secretary to the Governors, to arrive no later than 1 January.

Following allegations made in a recent television documentary, the Danby Clinic for Socially Embarrasing Diseases will be closed until further notice.

Major George Arnold has been asked to leave the SAS.

Peter Simmonds is being sued by AWG, the Brazilian chemical giant, for gross negligence.

Jane Sanderson wishes it to be known that although she did once have lunch with Mike Appleby, she has never had sexual relations with him in a lift at the top of the Empire State Building, and all rumours to the contrary are entirely without foundation.

Benefactions

Earlier this year the Society was left a very considerable sum in the estate of the late Mrs Josephine Bartlebottom. Under the terms of the will this bequest was to be held in trust, for so long as required, to provide for Fi-Fi Trixabel, a dachshund belonging to the deceased. The care of this animal was entrusted to the Governors of the Society.

Sadly, the dog was killed in a freak road accident two months ago. Fi-Fi Trixabel will be buried under the Society's new Josephine Barlebottom Memorial Theatre.

Professor Henry Jameson gave the Society a framed photograph of himself and his wife. It too will be buried under the Society's new theatre.

Sven Svenson has recently given a copy of his first book *Swedish Board Games of the Inter-War Period* to the library. It can be found in the new 'Swedish Board Games of the Inter-War Period' Section.

Appointments

Hamish McCloud replaces Arthur Botherington as Chairman of Governors at the start of the next non-academic year.

Philip Hatley and Susan Browning are the new Joint-Managers - of - Maintenance - and - Captains - of - Women's - Volleyball.

Jeremy Nuttington-Crisp Esq, Senior Archivist to the Society, and Director of the Oxbridge Reject Fine Art Commission, will be visiting his dentist at 2.30 pm next Friday.

Clubs and Societies

Women's Volleyball. It has been a disappointing year. We were disqualified from the league for including an old man in our team for some of our matches.

Men's Rugby. The excellent results of this season were largely overshadowed by one unfortunate incident. Four members of the squad missed a match after being arrested for causing 'extensive damage' to a restaurant in Swindon. Eventually the restaurant manager was located by the police and he was able to confirm that the four had indeed, as they claimed, been employed to re-fit the premises.

Athletics. Our Summer Sports Day was a great success this year, and a record number of records were broken. However, the event was slightly marred by the expulsions that resulted from the introduction of random drugs testing, and it is surely little compensation that those asked to leave the meeting were spectators and not participants. It was also sad, of course, that Ernest Thring of the Legal Department died during the day's final event. Next year we intend to introduce eye, hearing and agility tests for all judges in the Javelin Competition.

The Reject Drama Society is to perform Agatha Christie's baffling who-dunnit, *The Mousetrap*. Mrs Joan Bland will play the pretty Mollie Ralston, Dr Max Wormwood will be the neurotic Christopher Wren, and Steve Crozier has the part of the murderous Detective Sergeant Trotter.

The Light Opera Group (or The Gilbert and Sullivan Players) have postponed their performance of *The Pirates of Penzance* (or *The Slave of Duty*) because all copies of the libretto have been confiscated by the Department of Photocopying and Data Protection, which claimed that they were pirates.

The Debating Society's annual debate on the motion 'This House Believes That it *Is* in Control of its Own Destiny' was to have been proposed by the Countess d'Arling, and Henry Harrington Esq., and opposed by Lieutenant R. A. Berkeley, RN (Rtd), and Lord Justice Thring. Regrettably the debate has been cancelled owing to circumstances beyond our control.

Obituaries

Lieutenant Ronald Archibald 'Busby' Berkeley, RN (Rtd), Chairman of Governors 1981–86, died last year of a heart attack, aged sixty-nine. A memorial service was held on 12 December, 1989, at which Arthur Botherington, Chairman of Governors, delivered the following address:

'With 1989 drawing to a close, and Christmas nearly upon us, it is easy to forget that this year has not been without its share of sadness. I am thinking particularly of the untimely death of Busby Berkeley, whom we commemorate here today.

'The circumstances of Busby's death came as a great shock to many, particularly, of course, his lovely secretary; but it is some consolation that he was so very active right up until the end.

'When I took over from him as Chairman of Governors I was particularly conscious of the very large shoes that he had left behind for me to fill. I knew Busby for a good many years and quite apart from being a remarkably able Chairman, he was also a delightful golfing partner and a good friend.

'Born in 1918, Busby was by all accounts a loving and energetic child – characteristics which he retained until the day that he died. He was a good athlete at school, and went on to represent his university at the pole vault.

'The circumstances of our meeting are sufficiently unusual to bear repetition. I had been at the Annual Dinner of my university's Oxbridge Reject Society. Busby had also attended the Dinner, but had disappeared shortly after the soup together with two lady members who had been seated on either side of him. On returning to my rooms I became aware of a great noise issuing from them, and on entering expected to surprise a burglar. Instead I found Busby and his two young ladies playing leapfrog over one of the sofas, a considerable quantity of my brandy having already been consumed.

'Naturally we all became great friends and when both he and I joined the Navy shortly afterwards it was a happy chance that we found ourselves posted to the same ship. Needless to say, with Busby around our exploits – both aboard and ashore – were at times somewhat outrageous. It is a tribute to his valour and strength of character that, although he was never decorated, he was nonetheless mentioned in despatches to the Admiralty on several occasions.

'Following the war, Busby entered the family firm, which was soon to experience some considerable financial difficulty. It was Busby who was responsible for negotiating the company's sale to a larger firm of piston manufacturers, the proceeds of which he was to live on for a number of years.

'During the sixties Busby embarked on a number of relatively short-lived careers: he set up a consultancy firm, stood as a Parliamentary candidate and at one stage considered entering the Church. For a while he became an author and wrote two excellent, if somewhat ribald novels, sadly neither of which were published.

'It was then that the Oxbridge Reject Society invited him, like his father before him, to become Chairman of Governors, and certainly no more suitable candidate could have been found. Although Busby achieved a great deal as Chairman, he will be remembered best for his love of life. His friends will recall what he brought to the Society: generosity, a healthy enjoyment of life, and a big (if ultimately unreliable) heart.

'Although – somewhat to his regret – Busby never married, he was always a great ladies' man, a fact which gave added irony to the circumstances of his death. It is comforting, however, that he died as he had lived; gaining happiness through giving it to others.'

Lieutenant Ronald Berkeley, 1920–1989

Lord Justice Thring died earlier this year. The Legal Department has contributed the following appreciation:

Lord Justice Thring's career was one which attracted much controversy. From his first case as a judge, when he made legal history by imprisoning a man for non-payment of a blackmail demand, to his last in which he found himself in the dock, aged eighty-eight, accused of bringing the game of football into disrepute, Thring was never far from the headlines.

But it is not easy to assess Lord Justice Thring's contribution to the British legal system, not least because so many of his judgements were subsequently overturned.

Ernest Thring first caught the attention of the Society in 1920, the year in which he took Oxbridge. In his later years he was the first to admit that he acted rather rashly in threatening to sue Oxford University for not admitting him to study Law, but in those days he had yet to master the subject's intricacies.

Throughout his subsequent career, Ernest Thring was a devoted and valued member of the Society, and he was never happier than when his son failed Oxbridge just after the last war. Following his surprisingly early retirement, he became a leading light in the Legal Department, being largely responsible for the merging of the Mergers and the Acquisitions Divisions in 1978 (the year in which he became a Governor of the Society), and recently for the acquittal of the Treasurer on charges of insider dealing.

Ernest Thring was not a great sportsman and it is therefore rather ironic that he should die at an athletics meeting. However, he was an accomplished classicist, and if any member of the Society was to die by being impaled by a javelin, it seems right that it should be him.

Not only did Judge Thring give his best years to the Society, but he has, in death, donated his body to the Genetic Engineering Department. Although this has presently been mislaid by the post room, Lord Justice Thring will no doubt continue to serve the Society, in death as in life, once it is found.

Lord Justice Thring, 1901–1990

The Countess d'Arling died early in the New Year. The Treasurer writes:

If one sought to find any consistent pattern in the life of Countess d'Arling it must be that she developed the habit of outliving her husbands. Furthermore these husbands were, without exception, extremely wealthy, and by the time of her death the Countess – as she had become just ten months before – had accumulated a very considerable industrial holding and sat on the boards of no less than nineteen publicly-listed companies.

This is not to suggest that the Countess was anything less than a successful business-woman and entrepreneur in her own right. Immediately after leaving school and being rejected by Cambridge, Jane Montagu-Ruttington-Harper entered the fashion business. She had worked in her mother's fashionable Knightsbridge boutique for almost two weeks before meeting and subsequently marrying the industrialist Sir Hubert Shipton, some forty-eight years her senior.

When he died two years later, she looked around for something with which to occupy herself. She founded the Kensington and Chelsea Attractive Paper Doily Company, which over the next eighteen years she was to build up into a successful and profitable concern, with a nationwide reputation and a healthy clientele of small teashops. Meanwhile Lady Shipton, once plain Jane Montagu-Ruttington-Harper, had become Lady Ely upon her much publicized marriage to Viscount Ely.

When Lord Ely died, Lady Ely threw herself even more wholeheartedly into her business interests. In 1964 she founded the Oxbridge Reject Society's Women in Business Group, which had great success in placing her nieces in jobs with estate agents in Belgravia, and which she continued to chair right up until her death. Although she had sold the Kensington and Chelsea Attractive Paper Doily Company shortly after her second marriage, she still maintained a number of seats on boards, and worked tirelessly for charity and as a patron of the arts.

Lady Ely married Ronnie d'Arling, 13th Earl of Berkhampstead, in 1988, but their marriage was cut tragically short by his death in a jacuzzi, in mysterious circumstances, six weeks later.

Countess d'Arling was a remarkable, stout-hearted woman, whose character was strongly impressed upon the Society and she will be greatly missed.

The Countess d'Arling, 1912–1990

Henry Harrington died in July after a very short illness indeed. His son writes:

My father was devoted to the Society, which he joined shortly before the Second World War. His entry into the teaching profession was an unusual one – the family farm was losing money and it was Henry's idea to convert a number of the out-buildings into a boarding school for children between the ages of two and eighteen.

The school's radical start was to be reflected in many aspects of its life, and St George's was largely shaped by Henry's unusual educational theories, a lack of capital, and the need to milk four hundred cows twice a day.

In strictly educational terms, Henry Harrington was an exceptional head teacher. Fluent in almost two languages, he refused to have Classics taught in his school, and believed Science to be the 'language of the anti-Christ' – all the more surprising given his position as a confirmed atheist.

Although modern standards of tuition and cleanliness were by no means the fashion at the time, my father was insistent, all the same, that the boys should not be spoilt. Attention was not lavished on them, and one runaway once bicycled as far as Shanghai before his absence was noticed. But right up until the end, when the school inspectors finally won their closure order, my father remained convinced that though other schools might have higher educational standards, those at St George's were 'quite high enough', and that there was no need for such luxuries as central heating, libraries or qualified staff.

Despite my father's radical views his little school (and from the date that it was founded St George's did in fact grow smaller every year) produced some excellent academic results: an astonishing number of its pupils later failed Oxbridge, and in fact not a single one was ever admitted to either University.

My father contracted a serious illness after being struck by a fast-moving high-speed train. He died very shortly afterwards. He will be remembered affectionately by some of those who knew him.

Henry Harrington BA (pass), 1920–1990

Academic Results and Distinctions

In 1989 13,398 students distinguished themselves by failing Oxbridge.

The Roots of Rejection:
The Early Life of an Oxbridge Reject

Some of the most important recent developments in the field of psychology have arisen following the ground-breaking work on Oxbridge rejection by Dr Kurt Gunther, Consultant Psychologist to the Society, and himself an Oxbridge Reject. Here we publish his most recent contribution to the literature of the topic, in which he argues persuasively against the received view that Rejects are 'begotten not made'. This paper is a revised and extended version of this year's Reject Lecture, delivered to an enthralled audience at the Guildhall, in March.

Those approaching the debate for the first time should refer to the recent literature on the subject. See for example: *Oxbridge Rejection and its Impact on Early Aduthood*; Gunther & Wormwood (ORP 1981), *Abweisung in Oxbridge und die Kunst der Motorradwartung*; ed. Gunther (Deutsche Press, 1986), and *The Good, the Bad and the Hopeless; a Typology of Oxbridge Applicants*; Pegge (Milne Lecture, 1985).

The Roots of Rejection: Identifying and Understanding Significant Pre-Oxbridge Developments in Unsuccessful Applicants

Dr Kurt Gunther, M.A., Ph.D.

INTRODUCTION

The key question which any psychologist must ask when considering Oxbridge rejection is 'To what extent is rejection inherited? By contrast, is there any reason to suppose that the determining factors stem solely from the environment in which Rejects are reared? Is it necessary to postulate a combination of both 'nature' and 'nurture'? Is it in fact reasonable to assume that rejection or acceptance by Oxbridge is determined either by inherited or acquired determinators, or by some combination of both? Or is selection totally random and nothing to do with the psychology of the candidate at all?'

Of course the question is not as simple as this. What the research project described below does show, beyond any doubt, is that although we may be Oxbridge Rejects now, we were not just born Rejects.

We must therefore also ask the question, 'At what stage in the development process do Rejects develop the characteristics, skills and qualities which will later cause them to fail Oxbridge?' Our initial research was conducted with children aged between sixteen and eighteen. However, our original contention that factors relevant to rejection included laziness, differing examination conditions and inferior teaching methods was not confirmed.

For example, psychometric tests by Dr Wormwood and myself had indicated a tendency towards idleness among many Rejects, but methodological objections lodged by a number of highly respected researchers in the field have caused us to reconsider the significance of these results.

Another line of experimental enquiry failed to show that rejected candidates are given less time to sit the relevant examinations than those who are accepted, or that their interviews are generally shorter.

In addition, a project conducted by myself and Dr Olivia Pegge of the Statistics Department showed that in any given school a very high percentage of Rejects attend exactly the same lessons as successful Oxbridge candidates, suggesting strongly that there is very little or no difference in the way in which Rejects and acceptees are taught. Thus our original hypothesis had to be abandoned as untenable.

All existing evidence, therefore, indicated that the influences that lead to rejection develop much earlier than had at first been supposed. Our attention consequently switched to early infancy.

The Infant as Reject

In attempting to find the key to Oxbridge rejection while studying infants, we were presented with significant difficulties. The chief among these was that significant conclusions could only be drawn from infants who would subsequently become Oxbridge Rejects. This in itself posed two problems: identifying which infants would, in later life, apply to Oxbridge, and, of these, determining which would be rejected.

One solution to the first problem, proposed by Dr Wormwood and myself in 1963, can be termed Application Simulation.

Method One – Application Simulation

A group of 1000 infants, aged between six months and two years, was drawn at random from the population and each of these subjects was asked the following questions:

– What is your name?
– How old are you?
– Where is your mummy?
– Do you think that at some stage, perhaps between the ages of seventeen and nineteen, you will apply to Oxford or Cambridge University to further your academic studies?

The order of these questions was rotated in case the answer to one had some bearing on another.

One of the failings of this method was that it did not prove effective with subjects displaying poorly developed linguistic skills. In repeated tests on the youngest age group (6–8 months), for example, responses appeared to be random.

As a consequence, this first method of identifying future Oxbridge applicants was abandoned, and in June 1964 an alternative method was devised.

Method Two – Aspiration Prompting

The second method involved placing each infant alone in a comfortable, carpeted room containing two large photographs displayed at ground level, some distance apart. One picture was of a typical Oxbridge College whilst the other showed a photograph of a large pink fluffy bunny. Subjects were observed through a semi-mirrored panel and were categorized according to one of the following three behavioural patterns:

– subject crawled towards the Oxbridge College
– subject crawled towards the fluffy bunny
– subject did not crawl towards either photograph

In the majority of cases subjects crawled towards the fluffy bunny; fewer did not crawl to either photograph; only a small proportion moved towards the picture of the Oxbridge College.

Two very interesting observations could be made about the results of this experiment:

1. The proportion of the overall sample crawling towards the photograph of the Oxbridge College did not vary significantly even when the College depicted was changed.

2. The proportion of the overall sample crawling towards the photograph of the Oxbridge College was very similar to the actual proportion of the population within a given age group applying to Oxford or Cambridge.

Assessing Rejects

Having established which subjects were likely to apply to Oxbridge, it was then necessary to identify which would be rejected.

Method One (October 1964): Examinations

By this method, subjects sat the previous year's Oxford or Cambridge General Paper. The drawbacks of this experiment were found to be insurmountable since all examinees proved unable to read or write.

Method Two (November 1964): Interviews

By Method Two, each subject's suitability for Oxbridge was judged on their performance in interview, carried out by Oxbridge Admissions Tutors. Regrettably – despite assurances from all the Tutors concerned that they had taken into account age, maturity and level of academic work achieved –

every candidate failed (although three were referred to the pool, and one was encouraged to take nine months off and reapply the following year).

Method Three (January 1965–January 1984): Oxbridge
Method Three involved letting all subjects reach an age at which they could apply to Oxbridge in the usual fashion. This ensured that all subjects made the decision to apply to Oxbridge on the basis of cognitive development associated with their age and that the Admissions Tutors involved were able to make their decisions in accordance with actual rather than potential suitability.

Method Three was adopted in January 1965, and all other attempts to assess which of our subjects would fail Oxbridge were abandoned. Instead, a programme of monitoring pre-Oxbridge developments in infantile subjects was embarked upon, which was subsequently to be of great use in identifying the roots of Oxbridge rejection.

Data

Our total sample of 1000 infants was split into two age groups (6–12 months; 12–24 months) and tested in three key areas. These were:

1. Memory and Comprehension Tests
(a) *Memory Test*
Subjects were shown a number of common household objects as they passed on a conveyor belt and were then asked to recall to the experimenter what they had seen. Subjects were rewarded with chocolates according to the number of objects correctly remembered.
(b) *Comprehension Test*
Subjects were tested on their ability to name six objects from photographs. These photographs were: a dog; a house; a crown; an electron microscope; the species of sea urchin *Paracentrotus lividus*; a collapsing neutron star in the Galaxy Andromeda.

2. General Observation in a Play Scenario

In the second research area, groups of twenty subjects were introduced to a recreational scenario involving the following four play paradigms:

Swings
Climbing Frame
Sandpit
Seesaw

Each group was observed, and a film of the session was made for subsequent analysis.

3. Physiological and Personal Attributes

The following details were recorded:
(a) Age in months
(b) Size of feet
(c) Colour of eyes/whether glasses worn
(d) Number of pets kept in the family

Results

We are now able to present the results of this important study, drawing comparisons between the group of infants that took part in our experiments of 1965 and the adults they have become.

Of the total sample of 1000 infants, the breakdown of academic levels achieved is as follows:

Achieved one 'O' level or its equivalent 88.2%
Achieved one 'A' level or its equivalent 22.1%
Applied to a university 11.7%
Applied to Oxford or Cambridge University 1.0%
Accepted by Oxford or Cambridge University 0.2%

Clearly the samples involved when considering Oxbridge acceptance or rejection are not high: from our sample of 1000, ten applied and two got in. It is particularly important to note that the proportion applying is within one standard deviation of the proportion crawling towards the Oxbridge College in our 'fluffy bunny' experiment of 1964.

It is perhaps worthy of comment that it was a quite different ten infants who crawled towards the Oxbridge College to those who applied to Oxbridge in later life, suggesting that an intention to apply to Oxbridge in infancy makes it highly likely that such an application will not subsequently be made. It may, conversely, also suggest that an infantile interest in fluffy bunnies is conducive to Oxbridge application, but it is not possible to give statistical support to this hypothesis.

Analysis of Measures

1. Memory and Comprehension Tests

(a) The memory test was halted after a number of subjects' parents complained about the intake of chocolate involved and threatened to remove their children from the project.

(b) Recognition of objects from photographs was low. Forty per cent of those who later applied to Oxbridge identified the dog correctly, thirty per cent the house, and twenty per cent the crown. One future Reject identified the collapsing neutron star, but he did not specify which galaxy it was in, so this was not counted.

2. General Observation in a Play Scenario

Over the whole sample, the distribution of subjects onto the four different play paradigms was approximately even. However, when the later development of subjects was taken into account, analysis of the film revealed a clear pattern.

In particular a strong correlation was found between Oxbridge success and playing on a climbing frame, with exactly 100% of those subjects later accepted by Oxbridge gravitating towards this play scenario. Of the subsequent Rejects, 62.5% favoured the sandpit, whilst the other 37.5% spent the greater part of the session on the see-saw.

The film was shot without sound, and lip-reading experts have since been employed to analyze the level and content of the verbal interaction between individual subjects and their peers. There was a great deal of communication, but most appears to have been both random and unintelligible. This was particularly true of those who were to become Oxbridge Rejects, and may therefore be of use in helping to predict future performance in interview. This is a significant finding – and one to which we will return.

3. Physiological and Personal Attributes

(a) *Age in months*

As might have been expected, the proportion of subjects applying to Oxbridge from each of the two age groupings did not differ significantly, although the younger group almost without exception applied twelve months later than the older.

(b) *Size of feet*

Size of feet is an important factor; our findings showed quite clearly that the mean footsize of all subjects applying was significantly higher than the overall group mean, suggesting that this is a good indicator at a very early age. However, further investigation revealed that by the time the application was made, the foot size of the subjects involved was no longer abnormal. It should be noted that both subjects subsequently accepted by Oxbridge did have relatively small feet. Clearly there is scope for further research in this area in order to reach a working hypothesis.

(c) *Colour of eyes/whether glasses worn*

There was little or no evidence to suggest that eye colour had any bearing on either application or acceptance, and whilst all but one of the ten subjects applying to Oxbridge had been wearing glasses since at least 1973, there is no reason to suppose that this is anything more than a coincidence resulting from the small sample involved, and therefore has no bearing on our findings.

(d) *Number of pets kept in the family*

The significance of the 'pet factor' is hard to quantify. Some families who had kept no pets at the time of the initial experiments subsequently acquired some, whilst other families, who had previously kept several, lost one or more, either through bereavement or carelessness. In 1984 the whole sample was therefore contacted and asked whether they had been exposed to a family pet or pets at some stage during their lives, and if so, what animals these had been.

Those subjects who were rejected by Oxbridge were particularly likely to have been brought up at some stage in a family with a pet, and the mean number of pets in this group was significantly above the overall mean of 0.36, at 7.13 (it should be noted that this figure may be unusually high as one of the rejected subjects had spent their childhood on a farm with a Shetland pony, a donkey, three cats, seven dogs, nine horses, fifteen ducks and twenty-one geese).

Conversely, amongst those who were accepted by Oxbridge, the mean figure for family pet-keeping was well below the overall mean. Clearly then we can conclude that families with pets are significantly more likely to have a son or daughter rejected by Oxbridge, whereas those which do not keep a pet are more likely to have a child accepted by one or other of these Universities.

This is one of the most significant results of the study, with far-reaching implications both for the way in which Oxbridge candidates are appraised and for the Oxbridge Reject Society's own recruitment policy.

Conclusions

The research described demonstrates quite clearly that the roots of Oxbridge rejection can already be identified in infancy, and furthermore that these roots are the product both of the social world in which these infants are brought up, and of physiological characteristics inherited from their parents. The subtle interplay of physiology and psychology in shaping the infant Reject's relationships with its peers we have termed an 'Interlinear Multirelationship'.

The concept of an interlinear multirelationship represents a Gestalt shift from earlier theories, which not only subsumes the evidence arising from this study, but also allows us to account for all of the major stumbling blocks previously arising from research. Thus the Oxbridge rejection debate must move into a new domain. Previous deliberations about the supremacy of inherited over acquired attributes must give way to the new theoretical framework, and it is essential that previous misconceptions are abandoned if further research into this field is to prove productive.

It is now of paramount importance to concentrate on finding the connection between those factors that have already been identified as significant and to gain a clearer understanding of their relative importance within the Inter-linear Multirelationship. To correlate the separate and combined importance of these three elements it is necessary to undertake further research.

Dr Wormwood and I are therefore to embark on a major new project which will concentrate on monitoring infants' experiences on their first day at school. We will pay particular attention to the extent to which our subjects communicate with each other, the number of pets that they bring with them to school, and whether their feet grow significantly in the period between their first and last lesson. Our report, entitled *Oxbridge Rejection: Pet Theories*, will be published in approximately twenty years time.

Applying to Oxbridge

A Report by D. L. Goodhart,
Membership Secretary,
The Oxbridge Reject Society

To mark the recruitment of the 250,000th member to the ranks of the Oxbridge Reject Society, the Membership Department has produced the following report. This will help to remind Society members of the process of rejection – which probably took place very quickly and of which, no doubt, they remember little. It will also give some pointers to those who have yet to apply to Oxbridge, but who wish to acquaint themselves with the process of rejection before they do so.

Regrettably the Society is not granted a voting representative on the Oxford and Cambridge Collegiate Admissions Procedures Committees, so it is through no fault of our own that the process of application to Oxbridge seems to be in a state of flux.

I would like to be able to claim that I fully understand the differences between applying to the University of Oxford and the University of Cambridge, whether before, after, because of, despite, with, without, contingent upon or irrespective of 'A' level results. Alas, I cannot. I simply do not have the time to stay abreast of developments in this area, and for detailed information I must refer prospective members to our rival publications – the Oxford and Cambridge University Prospectuses.

In this period of rapid change, the Department is sometimes criticized for its policy regarding sabbatical leave (one year on, five years off). This is unfair. It is true that we no longer have a perfect grasp of the complexities of application, but I am pleased to be able to point out that this does not matter in the least. For while the application process may change, the rejection process remains very much the same.

Whilst compiling the report that follows, the Department

undertook to send questionnaires to sixty-five members of the Society – a Reject from every College at Oxford and Cambridge. The survey asked these Rejects about their experience of taking Oxbridge, and in particular anything that they could remember about the Ccollege to which they applied. I hope that the resulting information proves useful.

The responses to our survey show that the process of applying to Oxbridge involves four phases:

1. Filling in an application form
2. Sitting exams
3. Going for interview
4. Receiving a letter of rejection

Let us examine these in turn:

1. Filling in an Application Form

This is undoubtedly the most difficult hurdle in the application process. The two simplest ways for applicants to demonstrate unsuitability for Oxbridge are:

– to write their postcode at the end of their address and then notice the empty little box marked 'postcode'.

– writing today's date under 'date of birth'. [As recently published research has shown, it is possible for infants to express an intention to apply to Oxbridge, but it is rare for anyone under the age of thirteen to be admitted.]

Prospective applicants should also note that referees do not *have* to be games teachers.

It is also necessary to decide which of the sixty-five Oxford or Cambridge Colleges to apply to. The following table reflects individual opinions, but it is the Department's belief that they probably offer a reasonably accurate indication of the important differences between Colleges.

All Souls' College, Oxford
Rejecting Applicants Since: 1437
Strength: membership is regarded by some as the highest academic distinction in the world
Weakness: the College's name is misleading since it does not accept all souls

Number of Society Members Successful in Application: 0
Difficulty of Entry: 10
The College That Gave Us: Christopher Wren, architect

Balliol College, Oxford

Rejecting Applicants Since: 1263
Strength: the multi-gym has an excellent safety record
Weakness: the ratio of telephones to undergraduates is the lowest in Oxford
Number of Society Members Successful in Application: 0
Difficulty of Entry: 10
The College That Gave Us: Adam Smith, economist; Henry Smith, elliptic function theorist

Brasenose College, Oxford

Rejecting Applicants Since: 1509
Strength: the College operates a Target Schools scheme, encouraging large numbers of applicants
Weakness: all places are heavily over-subscribed
Number of Society Members Successful in application: 0
Difficulty of Entry: 10
The College That Gave Us: William Webb Ellis, clergyman and rugby player

Campion Hall, Oxford

Rejecting Applicants since: 1918
Strength: the tutors are all members of the Society of Jesus
Weakness: With just twenty-two students, it is perhaps a little on the small side
Number of Society Members Successful in Application: 0
Difficulty of Entry: 10
The College That Gave Us: Approximately seven Theology graduates a year

Christ Church College, Oxford

Rejecting Applicants Since: 1546
Strength: it's convenient for the Post Office
Weakness: the grandeur of the chapel would be more appropriate to a cathedral
Number of Society Members Successful in Application: 0
Difficulty of Entry: 10
The College That Gave Us: William Gladstone, Prime Minister and hand-luggage innovator

Christ's College, Cambridge

Rejecting Applicants Since: 1448

Strength: Anglo-Saxon, Norse and Celtic is taught by Dr V. A. Law

Weakness: the College is a friendly, welcoming and supportive community which encourages its members to combine academic work with other activities

Number of Society Members Successful in Application: 0

Difficulty of Entry: 10

The College That Gave Us: John Milton, poet and town-planner

Churchill College, Cambridge

Rejecting Applicants Since: 1960

Strength: the College Scarf is pink and brown

Weakness: the Henry Moore sculptures have holes in them

Number of Society Members Successful in Application: 0

Difficulty of Entry: 10

The College That Gave Us: a consistently good 'University Challenge' team

Clare College, Cambridge

Rejecting Applicants Since: 1326

Strength: Anglo-Saxon, Norse and Celtic is taught by Dr V. A. Law

Weakness: art exhibitions are sometimes held in the Latimer Room in Old Court

Number of Society Members Successful in Application: 0

Difficulty of Entry: 10

The College That Gave Us: Jane Carr, editor; Bishop Latimer, bishop

Clare Hall, Cambridge

Rejecting Applicants Since: 1966

Strength: it sounds more like a student than a College

Weakness: the Ashby Room only has space for eighteen people

Number of Society Members Successful in Application: 0

Difficulty of Entry: 10

The College That Didn't Give Us: a Pippard Bursary

Corpus Christi College, Cambridge

Rejecting Applicants Since: 1352

Strength: the College Library has the most reliable version of *The Saxon Chronicle* in existence

Weakness: sadly, it doesn't have the second most reliable version

Number of Society Members Successful in Application: 0

Difficulty of Entry: 10

The College That Gave Us: Hales' Hæmostaticks

Corpus Christi College, Oxford

Rejecting Applicants Since: 1517

Strength: it's named after a Cambridge College (presumably)

Weakness: unlike its namesake, it doesn't have *any* version of *The Saxon Chronicle*

Number of Society Members Successful in Application: 0

Difficulty of Entry: 10

The College That Gave Us: Thomas Arnold, rugby supporter

Darwin College, Cambridge

Rejecting Applicants Since: 1964

Strength: increases the chance of survival

Weakness: leads to extinction

Number of Society Members Successful in Application: 0

Difficulty of Entry: 10

The College That Gave Us: an opportunity to make a joke about 'The Origin of Species'

Downing College, Cambridge

Rejecting Applicants Since: 1800

Strength: College Croquet is usually played in accordance with Association Rules

Weakness: this means you're not allowed to put your foot on the ball

Number of Society Members Successful in Application: 0

Difficulty of Entry: 10

The College That Gave Us: little opportunity to send our opponent's ball into the far distance

Emmanuel College, Cambridge

Rejecting Applicants Since: 1584

Strength: the College has a very fine Bösendorfer

Weakness: some might hold that a Steinway would be preferable

Number of Society Members Successful in Application: 0

Difficulty of Entry: 10

The College That Gave Us: fewer than four Nobel Laureates this century

Exeter College, Oxford

Rejecting Applicants Since: 1314

Strength: graduate students are invited to dine with the Fellows at High Table once a term

Weakness: they are expected to accept

Number of Society Members Successful in Application: 0

Difficulty of Entry: 10

The College That Gave: its name to a whole University (presumably)

Fitzwilliam College, Cambridge

Rejecting Applicants Since: 1966

Strength: the admissions secretary is happy to respond to telephone and written enquiries

Weakness: there are fewer than five thousand books on International and Comparative Law and Political Science

Number of Society Members Successful in Application: 0

Difficulty of Entry: 10

The College That Gave Us: the Fitzwilliam Quartet, quartet

Girton College, Cambridge

Rejecting Applicants Since: 1869

Strength: the carp pond and the orchard

Weakness: the fish pie and the apple crumble

Number of Society Members Successful in Application: 0

Difficulty of Entry: 10

The College That Gave Us: good reason to eat elsewhere

Gonville & Caius College, Cambridge

Rejecting Applicants Since: 1348

Strength: it's easy to find

Weakness: it's difficult to spell

Number of Society Members Successful in Application: 0

Difficulty of Entry: 10

The College That Gave Us: Harold Abrahams, runner;
Titus Oates, perjuror

Green College, Oxford

Rejecting Applicants Since: 1979

Strength: accommodation, for students who are married,
is subject only to availability

Weakness: graduates are accepted for all science subjects,
including Biomathematics and Bioengineering, Forestry
and Applied Social Studies

Number of Society Members Successful in Application: 0

Difficulty of Entry: 10

The College That Gave: Biomathematics,
Bioengineering, Forestry and Applied Social Studies
graduates good reason to get married

Hertford College, Oxford

Rejecting Applicants Since: 1740

Strength: hurricanes hardly ever happen here

Weakness: it has only one Slavonic languages tutor

Number of Society Members Successful in Application: 0

Difficulty of Entry: 10

The College That Gave Us: Evelyn Waugh, parent

Jesus College, Cambridge

Rejecting Applicants Since: 1496

Strength: Anglo-Saxon, Norse & Celtic is taught by Dr
V. A. Law

Weakness: the College has not been Head of the River
for eleven consecutive years since 1885

Number of Society Members Successful in Application: 0

Difficulty of Entry: 10

The College That Gave Us: Archbishop Cranmer, Grand
Penitentiary of England and archbishop

Jesus College, Oxford

Rejecting Applicants Since: 1571

Strength: it's named after the Messiah (presumably)

Weakness: the Library hardly shuts at all

Number of Society Members Successful in Application: 0

Difficulty of Entry: 10

The College That Gave Us: Lawrence of Arabia, soldier;
Wilson of Rievaulx, prime minister

Keble College, Oxford

Rejecting Applicants Since: 1868

Strength: the new building has received an RIBA award

Weakness: as this implies, it is breathtakingly ugly

Number of Society Members Successful in Application: 0

Difficulty of Entry: 10

The College That Gave Us: the cheapest breakfast at any European higher educational establishment (with the possible exception of the University of Tübingen)

King's College, Cambridge

Rejecting Applicants Since: 1441

Strength: the high ratio of glass to stone in the chapel

Weakness: the high ratio of Fellows to Undergraduates in the College

Number of Society Members Successful in Application: 0

Difficulty of Entry: 10

The College That Gave Us: J. M. Keynes, economist and town-planner

Lady Margaret Hall, Oxford

Rejecting Applicants Since: 1878

Strength: the chapel choir gets a free dinner after Tuesday Evensong

Weakness: everyone else has to pay

Number of Society Members Successful in Application: 0

Difficulty of Entry: 10

The College That Gave Us: Princess Astrid of Norway, Norwegian princess

Linacre College, Oxford

Rejecting Applicants Since: 1962

Strength: the College rejects all those who apply to do undergraduate studies

Weakness: no one has ever heard of it

Number of Society Members Successful in Application: 0

Difficulty of Entry: 10

The College That Almost Gave Us: an anagram of 'Real Nice'

Lincoln College, Oxford

Rejecting Applicants Since: 1427

Strength: of all the Colleges at Oxford, Lincoln has the closest links with Switzerland

Weakness: it's nowhere near Lincoln

Number of Society Members Successful in Application: 0

Difficulty of Entry: 10

The College That Gave Us: Nathaniel, 3rd Lord Crewe, Bishop of Durham, bishop

Magdalen College, Oxford

Rejecting Applicants Since: 1458

Strength: the statue, in the tower, of William of Waynflete

Weakness: the statue, in the tower, of St Swithin

Number of Society Members Successful in Application: 0

Difficulty of Entry: 10

The College That Gave Us: Edward Gibbon, historian; Oscar Wilde, writer; Cardinal Wolsey, cardinal

Magdalene College, Cambridge

Rejecting Applicants Since: 1542

Strength: not named after Magdelen College, Oxford (presumably)

Weakness: (or, if it was, they spelt it wrong)

Number of Society Members Successful in Application: 0

Difficulty of Entry: 10

The College That Gave Us: Samuel Pepys, civil servant

Mansfield College, Oxford

Rejecting Applicants Since: 1886

Strength: the chapel has guest preachers on Wednesdays

Weakness: there is no Chemistry Tutor in the College (unless one happens to be preaching on a Wednesday)

Number of Society Members Successful in Application: 0

Difficulty of Entry: 10

The College That Gave Us: rather less than might have been expected

Merton College, Oxford

Rejecting Applicants Since: 1264

Strength: the College has the best food to be found in any European higher educational establishment (with the possible exception of the University of Tübingen)

Weakness: there is only one Real Tennis court

Number of Society Members Successful in Application: 0

Difficulty of Entry: 10

The College That Gave Us: a weight problem arising from too much to eat and not enough Real Tennis

New College, Oxford

Rejecting Applicants Since: 1379

Strength: the choir gives a very fine rendition of Handel's setting of the 'Te Deum'

Weakness: their Stanford in G could, however, benefit from a little more practice

Number of Society Members Successful in Application: 0

Difficulty of Entry: 10

The College That Gave Us: Tony Benn, Bennite

New Hall, Cambridge

Rejecting Applicants Since: 1954

Strength: its academic record is fairly solid

Weakness: its beds are not

Number of Society Members Successful in Application: 0

Difficulty of Entry: 10

The College That Gave Us: backache

Newnham College, Cambridge

Rejecting Applicants Since: 1871

Strength: students are not disturbed early in the morning by cleaners

Weakness: this is because there are no cleaners

Number of Society Members Successful in Application: 0

Difficulty of Entry: 10

The College That Gave Us: more vacuuming experience than one might have received elsewhere

Nuffield College, Oxford

Rejecting Applicants Since: 1937

Strength: there are only thirty Fellows

Weakness: all thirty are devoted to advanced study and research in social sciences

Number of Society Members Successful in Application: 0

Difficulty of Entry: 10

The College That Gave Us: nothing to eat during Christmas week

Oriel College, Oxford

Rejecting Applicants Since: 1326

Strength: there are five washing machines

Weakness: there are only four dryers

Number of Society Members Successful in Application: 0
Difficulty of Entry: 10
The College That Gave Us: Cecil Rhodes, imperialist;
Walter Raleigh, tobacconist

Pembroke College, Cambridge

Rejecting Applicants Since: 1347
Strength: imposing chimneys
Weakness: unimposing lavatories
Number of Society Members Successful in Application: 0
Difficulty of Entry: 10
The College That Gave Us: Harsnet's *Declaration of Egregious Popishe Impostures*

Pembroke College, Oxford

Rejecting Applicants Since: 1624
Strength: the College nurse is available every morning
Weakness: the College nurse is not available every night
Number of Society Members Successful in Application: 0
Difficulty of Entry: 10
The College That Gave Us: Samuel Johnson,
lexicographer

Peterhouse College, Cambridge

Rejecting Applicants Since: 1284
Strength: it's very old
Weakness: it's not as old as University College, Oxford
Number of Society Members Successful in Application: 0
Difficulty of Entry: 10
The College That Gave Us: Thomas Gray, elegist

Queens' College, Cambridge

Rejecting Applicants Since: 1448
Strength: Erasmus studied there in 1511
Weakness: he found the beer 'raw, small and windy'
Number of Society Members Successful in Application: 0
Difficulty of Entry: 10
The College That Gave Us: remarkably few people of
note, given that it's over five hundred years old

Queen's College, Oxford

Rejecting Applicants Since: 1341
Strength: members of the Eglesfield Musical Society
make up in enthusiasm what they lack in talent
Weakness: their enthusiasm is not very infectious

Number of Society Members Successful in Application: 0
Difficulty of Entry: 10
The College That Gave Us: Edmund Halley, cometator

Robinson College, Cambridge

Rejecting Applicants Since: 1977
Strength: the College continues to express its heartfelt
gratitude for the munificence of Sir David Robinson
Weakness: sadly the munificence of Sir David Robinson
did not extend to attractive buildings
Number of Society Members Successful in Application: 0
Difficulty of Entry: 10
The College That Gave Us: Barley Water

St Antony's College, Oxford

Rejecting Applicants Since: 1948
Strength: its location (it's in Oxford)
Weakness: it only has one strength
Number of Society Members Successful in Application: 0
Difficulty of Entry: 10
The College That Gave Us: nothing to write home about

St Benet's Hall, Oxford

Rejecting Applicants Since: 1918
Strength: it has the character of a Benedictine institution
Weakness: it *is* a Benedictine institution
Number of Society Members Successful in Application: 0
Difficulty of Entry: 10
The College That Gave Us: Benedictine monks with
degrees

St Catharine's College, Cambridge

Rejecting Applicants Since: 1473
Strength: it's named after a dock (presumably)
Weakness: many feel that, over the last few years, Catz
has gone to the dogs
Number of Society Members Successful in Application: 0
Difficulty of Entry: 10
The College That Gave Us: the Bangorian controversy

St Catherine's College, Oxford

Rejecting Applicants Since: 1963
Strength: the tourists avoid it
Weakness: the tourists are right
Number of Society Members Successful in Application: 0

Difficulty of Entry: 10

The College That Gave Us: little revenue from the sale of postcards

St Cross College, Oxford

Rejecting Applicants Since: 1965

Strength: the generous Emanoel Lee scholarships which the College offers

Weakness: the difficulty of getting one

Number of Society Members Successful in Application: 0

Difficulty of Entry: 10

The College That Didn't Give Us: an Emanoel Lee Scholarship

St Edmund Hall, Oxford

Rejecting Applicants Since: 1278

Strength: St Edmund Hall acquired full collegiate status in 1957, nearly 680 years after it was founded

Weakness: by this stage it was too late to change its name

Number of Society Members Successful in Application: 0

Difficulty of Entry: 10

The College That Gave Us: some of Arthur Frogley's finest cedar panelling

St Edmund's College, Cambridge

Rejecting Applicants Since: 1896

Strength: it has Approved Foundation status

Weakness: for years it didn't

Number of Society Members Successful in Application: 0

Difficulty of Entry: 10

The College That Gave Us: the Sea-Mammal Research Group

St Hilda's College, Oxford

Rejecting Applicants Since: 1893

Strength: it rejects all men

Weakness: it accepts only women

Number of Society Members Successful in Application: 0

Difficulty of Entry: 10

The College That Gave Us: a rather uneven male : female ratio

St Hugh's College, Oxford

Rejecting Applicants Since: 1886

Strength: the closing date for graduate scholarship

applications is 1 March

Weakness: this discriminates against graduates applying in non-leap years

Number of Society Members Successful in Application: 0

Difficulty of Entry: 10

The College That Gave Graduate Scholarship Applicants: cause to look forward to leap years

St John's College, Cambridge

Rejecting Applicants Since: 1511

Strength: it's very rich

Weakness: it not as rich as St John's College, Oxford

Number of Society Members Successful in Application: 0

Difficulty of Entry: 10

The College That Gave Us: Lord Palmerston, Prime Minister and gun-boat diplomat

St John's College, Oxford

Rejecting Applicants Since: 1555

Strength: it's very, very, very rich

Weakness: it hasn't got a swimming pool

Number of Society Members Successful in Application: 0

Difficulty of Entry: 10

The College That Gave Us: Robert Graves, dead poet

St Peter's College, Oxford

Rejecting Applicants Since: 1929

Strength: although the College is, at present, quite a long way from the top of the Norrington Table, this has only been the case for about sixty years

Weakness: the College recently celebrated its sixtieth anniversary

Number of Society Members Successful in Application: 0

Difficulty of Entry: 10

The College That Gave Us: a below average number of statisticians

Selwyn College, Cambridge

Rejecting Applicants Since: 1882

Strength: the two manual, tracker-action organ is by William Johnson & Son

Weakness: both manuals have gone missing

Number of Society Members Successful in Application: 0

Difficulty of Entry: 10

The College That Gave Us: John Selwyn Gummer, politician; Malcolm Selwyn Muggeridge, intellectual

Sidney Sussex College, Cambridge

Rejecting Applicants Since: 1596

Strength: Anglo-Saxon, Norse and Celtic is taught by Dr V. A. Law

Weakness: This is by no means an exclusive arrangement

Number of Society Members Successful in Application: 0

Difficulty of Entry: 10

The College That Gave Us: Oliver Cromwell, Lord Protector of England and Roundhead

Somerville College, Oxford

Rejecting Applicants Since: 1879

Strength: there's a creche

Weakness: students are not admitted

Number of Society Members Successful in Application: 0

Difficulty of Entry: 10

The College That Gave Us: Alison Clare, administrative supervisor

Trinity College, Cambridge

Rejecting Applicants Since: 1546

Strength: the Master of Trinity is appointed by the Monarch and the Prime Minster

Weakness: the Monarch and the Prime Minister are not appointed by the Master of Trinity

Number of Society Members Successful in Application: 0

Difficulty of Entry: 10

The College That Gave Us: the Earl of Sandwich, earl; Macaulay, Trevelyan and Carr, historians; Burgess, Philby, Maclean and Blunt, communist double agents

Trinity College, Oxford

Rejecting Applicants Since: 1554

Strength: the College has all the darts facilities you could reasonably wish for

Weakness: except for a decent darts board

Number of Society Members Successful in Application: 0

Difficulty of Entry: 10

The College That Gave Us: William Pitt the Elder, elder statesman

Trinity Hall, Cambridge

Rejecting Applicants Since: 1350

Strength: it attracts excellent Natural Science applicants

Weakness: it rejects many of them

Number of Society Members Successful in Application: 0

Difficulty of Entry: 10

The College That Gave Us: the only brass of Dr Hewke to be found in an Antechapel south of Ely

University College, Oxford

Rejecting Applicants Since: 1249

Strength: graduates of Oxford University applying for the Special Diploma in Social Studies are not required to submit GRE General Test scores

Weakness: graduates of other universities applying for the Special Dipoma in Social Studies *are* urged to submit GRE General Test scores if practicable

Number of Society Members Successful in Application: 0

Difficulty of Entry: 10

The College That Gave Us: the first Oxbridge rejection letter

Wadham College, Oxford

Rejecting Applicants Since: 1610

Strength: the gardens contain the finest tree in Oxford

Weakness: sadly, it is of little academic importance

Number of Society Members Successful in Application: 0

Difficulty of Entry: 10

The College That Gave Us: lots of jokes about left-wing students

Wolfson College, Cambridge

Rejecting Applicants Since: 1965

Strength: all the student rooms in the two principal College courts are wired up to the College computer network, which is in turn connected to the University Data Network and thence to other national and international networks

Weakness: the College's main strength is only of use to about three people.

Number of Society Members Successful in Application: 0

Difficulty of Entry: 10

The College That Gave Us: the best computer facilities to

be found in a European higher educational establishment (with the possible exception of the University of Tübingen)

Wolfson College, Oxford

Rejecting Applicants Since: 1966

Strength: the College runs a professionally-staffed day nursery

Weakness: the nursery is closed in the evening, so graduate students must, from 6 o'clock, play without supervision

Number of Society Members Successful in Application: 0

Difficulty of Entry: 10

The College That Gave Us: tears before bedtime

Worcester College, Oxford

Rejecting Applicants Since: 1714

Strength: there are two blocks of flats for married couples, one completed in 1974, and the other in 1978

Weakness: for four years the College had only one block of flats for married couples

Number of Society Members Successful in Application: 0

Difficulty of Entry: 10

The College That Gave Us: no blocks of flats for married couples until 1974

There are a number of colleges omitted from the above list, most of them intentionally. In particular no postgraduate teacher-training colleges have been included and it should be noted that attendance at one of these colleges does not disqualify Members from the Society. This is for two reasons: first, teacher-training colleges have traditionally been seen as independent bodies and, as a result of repeated representations from members, the Society continues to grant exemption. Secondly, teaching is a career targeted by the Society for Reject expansion, and the Careers Department is anxious that Rejects do not reject places at such colleges to avoid forfeiting their membership of the Society. If anyone has any confusion about eligibility, they should write to the Membership Secretary.

2. Sitting Exams

Many Rejects will have failed Oxbridge because they were given the following list of exam tips. It was first devised by a Membership Secretary at the turn of the century, and was widely circulated at the time – indeed it became something of a standard. Upon reading it, members will realize that it places absurdly high demands on the applicant – and is therefore bound to result in failure.

Tips for Exams
  i know your syllabus and revise the whole course thoroughly.
  ii Do not attempt to question spot – those who attempt it rarely succeed.
  iii Turn up on the right day, at the right time, and in the right place.
  iv Make sure that you have the correct paper in front of you.
  v Be sure to turn over the paper – there may be questions printed on the back.
  vi Read each question three times, with intelligence.
  vii Follow the instructions carefully and answer the correct number of questions. You cannot be awarded marks for a question you have not attempted.
  viii Divide your time according to the proportion of marks allotted to each question.
  ix Try not to be influenced by those sitting next to you.
  x Do not cheat – you will get caught.

Since the above list was developed, examinations have become a less important element of the Oxbridge admissions procedure. To encourage still more people to apply, therefore, the Department has been developing a new, more realistic set of tips. It is anticipated that these will make less exacting and more practicable demands on candidates.

Revised Tips For Exams
  i know as much of your course as time allows and cram

feverishly as the hours run out.

ii Do question spot – if you weren't meant to, it wouldn't work.

iii Turn up late – you'll avoid the awful tension created by fellow examinees discussing parts of your course that you never knew existed.

iv If you find that you have the wrong exam paper in front of you, read it before you complain. It might be easy.

v If things are looking bad, do not answer any questions on the back of the paper and claim later that (a) you did not know that they were there and (b) that they were the questions you would have chosen.

vi If time is pressing, it is probably enough to read each question once with a modicum of common sense. If time is nearly up, seconds spent reading questions are seconds wasted.

vii In an emergency either write illegibly, or don't hand anything in and blame the examiners for losing your answer paper.

viii Divide your time according to the amount that you can write on any given question.

ix Try not to be influenced by those committing suicide next to you. The examiner will find them at the end of the exam.

x Cheat if you have to – you may get away with it.

This prototype list of exam tips is still undergoing field tests, but when it is ready it will be forwarded to schools, where it is expected to become the new standard.

3. Going for Interview

This is an optional stage. Many candidates will bypass it, but for those that do not it can be the most time consuming.

Many people believe that the quickest route into Oxford or Cambridge is to astonish the interviewer into noticing them. This popular supposition arose as a result of a highly successful campaign of misinformation, instituted by the Society's Membership Secretary in the 1930s.

This misleading advice was instrumental in raising the Society's membership to record levels, and older members of the Society (including many past and present officers) have stories testifying to its inaccuracy.

Tales are related of Rejects at interview who insisted upon singing all their answers, replied entirely in rhyming couplets, or, as in my own case, refused to answer any of the questions asked on the grounds that they were 'far too easy'.

Our last Treasurer, having failed to attract attention during an interview with a theology professor by appearing to have a religious experience, resorted to pretending to suffer a stroke. Some years before, his uncle – a former Chairman of Governors – had distinguished himself by sending a messenger to his interview with a note of absence, claiming that he was, at the time, engaged upon top secret work for His Majesty's Government which prevented him from disclosing his whereabouts, and would they please let him in anyway. They did not.

Perhaps the most celebrated interview concerned an applicant who was invited by the Admissions Tutor to find some method of gaining his attention. The applicant took out a box of matches and set light to the interviewer's jacket, causing him second degree burns and considerable damage to the College.

Unfortunately the story has an unhappy ending, since the same individual re-applied the following year to another College. At interview, he was again encouraged to attract attention, and this time, because the Admissions Tutor was not wearing a jacket, he showed the presence of mind to set light to the newspaper that the interviewer was reading at the time. On the strength of this demonstration of flair and imagination, he was awarded an unconditional offer.

Following this incident the student involved had to resign from the Society. The policy of inciting high-profile interview techniques was abandoned shortly thereafter.

4. Receiving a Letter of Rejection

The fourth phase in any application to Oxbridge is the simplest. Applicants who have completed the preliminary stages will receive, usually just before Christmas, a letter from an Oxford or Cambridge college containing not seasonal greetings, but an explanation as to why their further education will take place elsewhere.

The only thing that an applicant has to do on receipt of such a letter is to open it and read it.

Members may be interested to note that this phase in the application process is not only the most straightforward, but also the oldest. Rejection letters have, in point of fact, remained almost unchanged in form and content for 700 years. This can clearly be seen from an examination of the first-ever rejection letter, which is held in the Society's archive:

collegio academiae,   Kal. Dec. a.d. MCCXLIX
Oxoniensis, OXI IVBI

me paenitet te certiorem facere nos sedem ullam buius collegii tibi offere non posse. fortasse possit fieri ut petitionem tuam accipiat collegium aliud, sed in maximam spem adduci inconsultus sis, quod, ut planius dicam, aliud non est adhuc conditum.

nihilominus, haud dubium est quin multum vero consecutus sis quippe paene ascenderis ultimum gradum eius certationis quae hoc anno ardissima esse videatur.

mox autem epistolam recipies quae tibi amplius exponere quomodo peregisti.

vale,

Guillamus de Gaillia,
praeceptor admissionum

A translation of the above reads as follows:

University College,   1 December, 1249.
Oxford, OX1 4BJ.

I am sorry to have to tell you that we shall not be able to offer you a place at this College. It is still just possible that your application may be considered by other Colleges, but it would be wrong, I am afraid, to hold out much hope, because there are no other Colleges.

This year the competition was very stiff and you did particularly well to reach this stage.

Before long the College will be writing to you to comment further on your performance.

Yours faithfully,

William de Gale,
Tutor for Admissions

Having read such a letter, and providing, of course, that the candidate shall, at no time previously, have either obtained a degree from a College at Oxford or Cambridge, or committed primaticide, the recipient becomes a full member of the Oxbridge Reject Society, and can enjoy all the historic rights and privileges that this entails. Members may wear the Society Tie and Brooch, are exempted from paying beard tax, and can enjoy a substantial reduction on the purchase of Holy Relics in the Duchy of Cornwall, between Whitsun and the Feast of St Boniface.

The Reject at University
With An Introduction by Steven Crozier,
Universities Representative

The Oxbridge Reject
Society

From the Universities Representative

Dear Oxbridge Rejects,

Steve Crozier is my name for those of you that don't
know me - which can't be too many of you seeing as I've
been Universities Rep since the year dot.

My role, as I see it, is one of liaison and motivation.
Liaison with the Oxbridge Reject Society branches at
universities throughout the UK, and motivation at
branch committee level to organise events and encourage
Rejects to become active members of the Society. My
priorities are frequent visits to the branches and
regular dialogue sessions with key personnel, as such.
These, I have found, can be highly motivating as well
as providing a useful opportunity for strategic and
tactical planning, both proactive and inactive.

In addition to these individual meetings, I also
regularly invite all branch presidents and their
deputies to an annual workshop weekend. The idea being
is that this is an ideal opportunity for branches to
touch base, and bring the less motivated up to speed.
There are also syndicate sessions where grievances can
be aired and challenges (I don't believe in the word
'problems') can be discussed. All in all, it can be
very stimulating for everyone, actually.

This year we've had one of the best turn-outs for the
workshop that I can remember, and I'd like to take this
opportunity of thanking everyone who came, particularly
the lovely Karen and not forgetting Barry (one or two
jars too many, eh Baz?!). Once again we were right
royally looked after by the Clara Hotel, Harrogate, to

who we record our gratitude here.

All in all it's been a good year for me. As
Universities Rep I cover a fair few miles _per annum_, of
course, and I also see a goodly number of people from
all over the country in the course of the job - most of
them Oxbridge Rejects. For this reason I've always
slightly regretted that I was not an Oxbridge Reject
myself. When I first started working for the Society I
used to think it didn't make too much difference, but
in the end I decided I had to hand it to Oxbridge
Rejects. There's something that sets us slightly
apart. I say 'us' because I am proud to be able to
tell you that earlier this year, thanks to the
Membership Secretary who encouraged me, I became an
Oxbridge Reject myself. I need hardly tell you that it
was the proudest moment of my professional and personal
career and I would like to thank all of my colleagues
who were so supportive and helped me fill in the
application form.

It's been a good year for the grass root branches too.
But they can do a much better job than I can in filling
you in on what's been going on in the universities in
the last twelve months. So I'll take this opportunity
to sign off.

Cheers.

Steve Crozier,
Universities Representative,
The Oxbridge Reject Society

1. Bristol University: A report from Karen Black, President, BOReS

Our biggest project this year was the instigation of a series of lectures held in the Victoria Rooms. With Steve Crozier's help we were able to obtain for the first lecture Dr Olivia Pegge, of the Society's Statistics Department, who gave a two-hour lecture entitled: 'A Short Statistical Analysis of Oxbridge Rejects at the University of Bristol, 1931–1933'.

It is a tribute to the efforts of our Publicity Officer that attendance was almost capacity, with nearly 700 people in the audience – the majority of them from outside the university. Unfortunately most were not able to stay to the end of the lecture, and many missed Dr Pegge's fascinating exposition on how she initially set about conducting her research. As they left, one or two did mention that they had been given to understand that the talk was to be on the subject 'Self-fulfillment through Copulation', and indeed this was the title which had been advertised in the previous day's *Bristol Evening Post*. We can only assume that this was a mistake, since our Publicity Officer assures us that she sent them the correct details.

Later, in the Mandela Bar, Dr Pegge congratulated us on our initial turnout, which she said she had calculated was over a hundred times larger than at her last lecture, and she kindly bought all the remaining members of the audience a drink.

We are now looking forward to the forthcoming lecture by the Society's Rejectus Professor of Modern History, Mathew Donaldson, entitled: 'Oxbridge Rejects from Bristol and Avon in the Franco-Prussian War'. It should be noted that the subject of this talk has been incorrectly advertised in *Epigram*, the *Journal* and the *South Avon Mercury* as 'The Joy of Sado-Masochism'.

2. Durham University: A report from Rupert Squirrel, President, DOReS

Despite being moved from our promised stand in the Mandela Ballroom and ending up in the laundry, we had a record intake of members at Societies Day in Dunelm this year. This was largely because we were offering each new recruit a specially-concocted and rather potent cocktail called – appropriately enough – an Oxbridge Reject. This owed quite a lot to curaçao, which gave it a reasonably accurate Cambridge blue colour, and was decorated with an Oxford blue cocktail umbrella. Unfortunately at one point the Treasurer, Clare, managed to knock a pile of cheques into the mixing vat, but we turned the unfavourable position to our advantage and dried them in the tumble drier. The only painful consequence was the bank manager's endless comments about the Society laundering money.

Otherwise we have had a number of social events. Our October disco at the Buffalo Head was surprisingly ill-attended – those who did come had a highly memorable evening and both bought each other several rounds of drinks before finally being persuaded to move elsewhere. By contrast our 'Eve of Examinations' party was, if anything, too full. This was largely because, rather than holding it prior to the university exams in late May, this year it was moved to October and the eve of Oxbridge exams. As a novelty, before gaining admittance to the event members were asked to undergo a short interview of an unusually searching nature conducted by the Vice-President and Secretary of the Society dressed up as Oxbridge Admissions Tutors. Those who were thought to have shown a particularly poor performance were given a free glass of the now celebrated Oxbridge Reject cocktail. Unfortunately, we had to award so many of these free drinks that the bar made a significant loss.

3. Edinburgh University: A report from Barry Armstrong, President, Edinburgh Independent Oxbridge Rejects Association

This is our last report, because earlier this month at the Annual General Meeting our members voted overwhelmingly in favour of disaffiliation from the main body of the Society. This will have two beneficial effects: we will gain total independence from the national Oxbridge Reject Society in all our decision-making processes, and we will be spared endless visits from the insufferable Steve Crozier.

For the record, our main event this year was a sponsored charity race to Oxford and Cambridge in aid of their appeals. There were eight entrants, all of whom were sponsored by friends to race to the Oxbridge College which had rejected them, pose for a photograph of themselves holding a copy of that day's newspaper while shaking hands with the College's Admissions Tutor, and return to Edinburgh. All eight set out simultaneously from the Mandela Centre on a cold March morning with just ten pounds in their pockets. Four were heading towards Cambridge, three to Oxford, and one, who had applied to both Universities, was attempting to reach the midpoint between the two – Milton Keynes.

Paul, JJ, Anna T-C and Patrick all clubbed together, bought one rail ticket to London and spent nearly five hours hiding together in a toilet as it travelled south at 125 miles per hour. When they arrived they decided that they had probably spent enough time together and split up.

Paul and Anna T-C went straight to Paddington and got on a train to Oxford without a ticket, hoping that the ticket inspector would understand when they explained that it was all for charity. Unfortunately they were arrested, spent a night in the cells, and were later awarded criminal records by a magistrate who turned out to be the Admissions Tutor of the College Paul had applied to. JJ went to his father's firm and got the chauffeur to drive him to Cambridge, but when he arrived the College Admissions Tutor refused either to pose for a photograph or shake his hand. While travelling across London, Patrick met a couple of his sister's friends on the tube, and when they invited him to a party he decided to drop out of the race.

Big Anna spent her ten pounds on the train fare to RAF Leuchars and managed to talk her way onto a routine flight to RAF Abingdon. Unfortunately for her, because of bad weather, the flight was diverted to RAF Duckworth so she decided to go to Trinity College, Cambridge rather than Trinity College, Oxford for her photograph. If the rules of the competition had not been so strict, Big Anna would have won, since she was able to beg a return flight from her new RAF friends and was back in Edinburgh early the same evening. Nonetheless, the Committee wishes her every happiness in her forthcoming marriage to Flight Lieutenant Giles Holdsworth.

James and Claire had the idea of approaching a car rental firm, explaining the situation, and offering to drive any of their vehicles south. They were given a small van, with a full tank of petrol, and arrived at the company's depot at Heathrow twenty-two hours later. They proceeded to the City where each had arranged first interviews with eight merchant banks. This left them with almost £1,600 in reimbursed travelling expenses, which they used to charter a plane from City Airport. They flew to Cambridge, had their photographs taken, and then flew on to Edinburgh, where they were greeted as the joint winners.

Nigel Maynard, who set out for Milton Keynes, has not returned.

4. Exeter University: A report from Jamie McCloud, President E-OReS

This year has seen the election of several new officers, including myself as President, following the retirement of a number of third years to concentrate on finals. One of our first moves has been to meet much more regularly, and our meetings in the Nelson Mandela Room now take place twice a term. We have already set about initiating a number of new activities and schemes, including new ways to boost revenue.

Our biggest coup was to introduce, during rag week, the

Oxbridge Reject 'hit'. This involves a distinguished old Oxbridge don rushing into a lecture to inform the victim that there has been a terrible mistake, that they have in fact been accepted by their chosen College at Oxford or Cambridge, and that unless they put in an appearance before the end of the day, they will be sent down, forfeiting their place. The don then bundles the victim into a waiting car and drives them blindfold to the College to which they applied years previously, leaving them gagged and bound in the middle of the quad.

Proceeds from these hits were to have been donated to the appeals of Oxford and Cambridge Universities. Unfortunately the sums involved in defraying the expenses of the distinguished old don proved to be higher than expected. He incurred substantial costs travelling between Exeter and his home, and combined with the outlay in rewarding him with a case of Château Pichon-Longueville, Comtesse de Lalande 1961, total expenditure almost exceeded our revenue and indeed would have done, had we taken into account the expense of posting the cheques.

5. London University: A report from Jenny Spinner, President LOReS

The University of London Oxbridge Reject Society Committee has a large number of highly active sub-committees, which devotedly meet in most college JCR's twice every weekday for an hour at lunchtime and again in the late afternoon. Unfortunately the anticipation, watching and subsequent discussion of Australian soap-operas has figured largely in this timetable, and as a consequence we have achieved little this year.

6. Manchester Univeristy: A report from Francis Petherick, President, MOReS

This year we decided to concentrate all our efforts on one big social event in the Steve Biko Building. This was to be based around a screening of the *Rocky Horror Picture Show* in the MDH, followed by an Oxbridge Reject Bop for which we applied for a late licence. However, our new Social Secretary was worried that the event might not be a success and decided to do a little market research, on the basis of which he cancelled the whole event having discovered that most people had already seen the film.

As a result of the fact that two terms of planning had come to nothing, we found ourselves with very little to report in our newsletter. Consequently we decided, at the last moment, to turn it into an arts magazine for one issue. This proved a very popular move, and a number of members contributed work at short notice. This ranged from a detailed critique by a second-year English student of David Spratt's cult, silent film *Idyll*, to a moving photographic portrait, in black and white, of English students at work in the John Rylands university library, entitled 'English Students at Work in the John Rylands University Library'.

In addition, there were a number of excellent poems submitted, one of which we feel deserves to be reprinted here:

> the photographer clicks
> his camera
> stillness in motion
> (verisimilitude)
>
> he looks
> and sees again
> what he photographs
>
> movement
> english students at work
>
> in a library
>
> in manchester
>
> the camera (poet
> ry in motion)
> idyll of language (still)
> snap snap snap
>
> SNAP by
> KENNETH TATE

7. St Andrews University: A report from Tarquin Nuttington-Crisp, President, StOReS

St Andrews has the oldest university Oxbridge Reject Society in the country, and this year we celebrated our five hundred and seventy-ninth anniversary. We were again very pleased to welcome the Society's Chairman of Governors, Arthur Botherington as Guest of Honour at our annual dinner. Sadly, last year's venue, as we had been expecting, proved to be unavailable, but the Atholl Palace, Pitlochry, layed on an excellent evening, and it is to be regretted that the hotel's manager has written to inform us that they will not be able to accommodate us next year.

The highlight of the evening was undoubtedly the opportunity to enjoy once again the Chairman of Governor's considerable gift as an after-dinner speaker. Those who attended the dinner last year were able to testify that none of his amusing anecdotes had lost anything in the retelling.

It was a great pity that such a memorable occasion was slightly marred by two separate motoring incidents: the Secretary was most unfortunate to encounter an unusually large stag whilst returning the Chairman to the Russack's. His evasive action was both swift and sensible, so it was therefore extremely unlucky that his Golf convertible careered off the road in an uncontrollable spin and landed upside-down in a ditch. We are particularly thankful that all seven passengers were able to emerge unhurt. By comparison the second incident was relatively slight and the Assistant Treasurer was discharged from Ninewells Hospital within a matter of weeks. It was very fortunate for him that the other vehicle involved in the collision happened to be an ambulance.

We were particularly delighted that, although the Chairman of Governors had feared he would not – as in previous years – be able to stay with us for a few days, he resolved on arrival not to return South to attend a number of departmental meetings and the funerals of two old Society friends. He was therefore able to remain an extra fourteen days. Given his original plans, it was lucky that he had thought to bring with him a full set of golf clubs, his spikes, and a remarkable collection of his grandfather's tartan plus-fours.

8. York University: A report from Rachel Pegge, President, YOReS

Please excuse a rather short report – I've got a massive essay crisis, so I haven't much time. I've included a copy of the minutes of our last meeting which should offer a pretty good guide as to what's been going on up here at York.

Minutes of a meeting of the York Oxbridge Reject Society held on 6 March at 8.15 pm in Derwent College Bar.

(i) Minutes of the last meeting
  The minutes of the last meeting were distributed in advance. At the meeting they were duly ratified, after the Secretary promised to correct the spelling of Mr Ibbotson's name on the sixteen occasions that it appeared in the minutes.

(ii) Matters arising
  The Custodian reported that the four stuffed cockatoos and the wheel clamp had now been returned.

(iii) The trip to Castle Howard
  The Secretary reported that the trip to Rievaulx Abbey and Castle Howard had been a great success and had even made a small profit. Everybody enjoyed the day out, and it was very much hoped that it could be repeated next year.

  Mr Ibbotson (Vanbrugh) asked the Secretary whether it might be possible to organise next year's event for slightly later in the term, since his umbrella had been largely destroyed in the blizzard. The Secretary agreed that this might be a sensible move.

  The Treasurer announced that she had received a letter from Continental Coaches of Nelson Street, apologising for the breakdown of the coach and for the delays in getting a replacement, but regretting that it would not be possible to offer a reduction in the cost of hire owing to the unusual expenses incurred in cleaning both coaches. They went on to point out that although, as they had discussed with the Treasurer, they would be pleased to operate a vehicle for another such event next year, they would have to insist that alcohol was not consumed on the coach, and that no one should embark whilst insensible from having imbibed to excess. In particular they would ask that Mr Crozier did not come in future, in case a similar incident should occur with the door of the emergency exit whilst the coach was in motion.

Mr Ibbotson asked that a comprehensive list and a more careful count of passengers be made before departure from the stops, since he had been caused considerable inconvenience in being left at Rievaulx Abbey. Miss Grant (Vanbrugh) echoed this point, pointing out that she was particularly annoyed to have been left behind, because she had gone to some trouble to tell the Social Secretary that she was going to look for Mr Ibbotson. The same point was raised by Miss Colefax (Vanbrugh), Mr Ali (Vanbrugh), Mr Thompson (Vanbrugh) and Miss Barnwell (Vanbrugh).

Miss Chapel (Wentworth) told the Publicity Officer that she had been led to believe that the coach would be returning to York by 5.30 p.m. She pointed out that the expedition's publicity had made no mention of a four-hour return journey, and asked whether, next time, it might not be possible to take a map.

(iv) Any other business

Mr Ibbotson raised the point that it semed rather unfair that the Society always met in Derwent College Bar and could the next meeting take place at Vanbrugh College Bar where he was sure that the Society would meet with a warm welcome? The President thanked him for his kind invitation, but regretted that details had already been sent out, so it was too late to make changes. Mr Ibbotson commented that this was what he had said last time.

(v) Date of Next Meeting
   8.15 p.m., 14 May, Derwent College Bar.

No other University Oxbridge Reject Societies have submitted reports this year.

Courses at University

This section, compiled by the Department of Education's Board of Reject Studies, offers advice to any Reject unsure about what to study at university, and may also be of interest to Rejects who left higher education some years ago and cannot clearly remember what their course involved.

English

Oxbridge Rejects feel at home with English. For a start, it is usually their first, and in many cases only, language. Furthermore they don't feel self-conscious about their own literary shortcomings. If challenged they can find justification for almost any fault, pointing out that both Chaucer and Shakespeare were highly inconsistent about spelling, Joyce's grammar is suspect, Beckett seemed unable to master the rudiments of plot construction, and even Enid Blyton can be charged with poor characterization.

French

Oxbridge Rejects are immediately attracted to French because of its joie de vivre, its esprit de corps and because it is so chic. On starting the course, however, they discover that they are expected to study French medieval literature and become seriously disaffected.

Many students of French fully expect that they will spend their year abroad either entering café society in Paris or skiing in Meribel, so they are almost invariably a little saddened to find themselves en route to a small industrial town a few kilometres from Clermont Ferrand.

German

Rejects studying this course have no difficulty in placing verbs at the end of the sentence, giving capital letters to nouns and stringing numerous short words together to make long ones. This comes in very useful when they start learning German.

By the time that Rejects reach university they are usually approaching fluency in German and are looking forward to a year spent abroad studying the language in more depth. For this reason it comes as rather a disappointment to find that all Germans speak excellent English, and that their efforts were therefore something of a waste of time.

Russian

Until recently, Russian has not enjoyed great popularity with Oxbridge Rejects, most of whom become noticeably bolshie when asked to learn a new alphabet. To compound this problem, Russian literature is remarkable for the number of extremely long books which it has produced.

However Russian is now enjoying something of an increase in popularity amongst Rejects, which can only be regarded as a steppe in the right direction.

Classics

Classics is all Greek to Oxbridge Rejects.

Theology

Theology is not a university course favoured by Oxbridge Rejects, dealing as it does with abstract concepts. Rejects are reluctant to consider carefully the existence of God; having failed Oxbridge they are unsure of their entitlement to salvation, and live in fear of receiving a letter of Rejection on the Day of Judgement.

Those Rejects who do study Theology are divided into two schools of thought: the fatalists who believe that their failing Oxbridge was pre-ordained, and the nihilists who believe that the entrance examinations, the interviews, the letter of rejection and indeed the College itself are all figments of someone else's imagination, placed there by an evil demon.

Philosophy

It is open to question whether Oxbridge Rejects can ever be said to *be* philosophers, but it seems reasonable to assert that some at least are thinking about it. Hence, if:

OR is equivalent to the statement 'is an Oxbridge Reject'
P is equivalent to the statement 'is a philosopher'
T is equivalent to the statement 'is thinking about being a
philosopher'

then we see that for x to be OR and for x to be P then x
must be T and T must be equivalent to P or OR must be
not equivalent to P if OR is equivalent to T or if OR is
equivalent to not T unless not T is equivalent to P. But
since T is not equivalent to P, consequently we can
conclude that Oxbridge Rejects *can* be philosophers without even thinking about it. Hence we see that if Descartes
had been an Oxbridge Reject he would have had to have
stated 'I think therefore I am not'.

PPP
This course is not available to Oxbridge Rejects.

Politics
Oxbridge Rejects are at liberty to study politics, and many
elect to do so of their own free will. As a result, members of
the Society are proportionally well-represented in Politics
Departments throughout the country. But although Politics
is a subject in which Rejects can excell, most have trouble at
Mill, many never find the key to Locke, and few finish first
past the post.

PPE
See PPE

History
Having studied History at 'A' level, Rejects arrive at university expecting to study important events and dead statesmen.
They are therefore often somewhat surprised to discover
that their course contains almost nothing except trivial
debates about living historians.

Furthermore, the old adage that 'history never repeats
itself' would appear to imply that the syllabus is impossibly
large. Happily Oxbridge Reject and Oxbridge graduate
historians alike soon evolve the standard response 'Not my
period' whenever faced with a bit of history which has never
previously been repeated to them.

The secret of History, then, is to deflect all discussion onto the merits, or otherwise, of living historians, whilst constantly honing one's own area of specialization so that it comes close to vanishing altogether. This is not really a reliable exam technique, but it is the simplest way to survive at parties when asked about your course.

Economics

The key to Economics lies in the assumption that it is all right to make assumptions. Although there may be grounds for supposing that this is a rather uncertain basis upon which to build a science, this is not something which seems to worry Oxbridge Rejects any more than other economists, and for this reason Rejects are well suited to the subject.

Economics works because of the old adage that 'history always repeats itself'. From this premise, complex economic theories can be developed which, by making predictions based on what has occurred previously, will eventually prove that history does indeed always repeat itself.

If, on the other hand, it is found that these predictions are wrong, this is for one of three reasons:

1. A different bit of history should have been used to formulate the complex economic theory
2. The complex economic theory was not complex enough
3. History does not, after all, repeat itself

Because they necessitate starting again from scratch, answers 1 and 2 are not appealing to Oxbridge Rejects, and they turn to 3. This has led to the emergence of two opposing Reject theories of economics. One states that 'In an ideal world, *omnis paribus* (all things being equal), there will be no variables and everything can therefore be predicted with absolute accuracy, the answer being constant'.

The opposing view is that since the world is not ideal, but has infinite variables, nothing can be predicted, anything could happen and therefore that 'One should not make assumptions'.

Law

The study of Law is offered at universities as a deterrent to anyone thinking about helping themselves to a share of the financial rewards enjoyed by those already in this profession. There is little compensation for the fact that the subject is supremely tortuous, to the point of being criminal, and completely divorced from reality.

Although Law cannot be advocated as likely to appeal to Oxbridge Rejects, nonetheless it is a subject to which a surprising number find themselves condemned. Law suitability must be left to individual Rejects to judge.

Archaeology, History of Art and Computing

With the growing awareness of ecological issues, Rejects have been increasingly less inclined to take courses involving preservatives, colouring, and artificial intelligence.

Geography

Geography is one of the most popular subjects with Oxbridge Rejects who are attracted by the possibility of obtaining a degree in a subject concerned with depression, erosion, meanders and faults.

Mathematics

Oxbridge Rejects tend to be attracted to Mathematics because it is precise, elegant and the answers are in the back of the book.

On the whole, Rejects prefer Pure Mathematics to Applied, because they associate the word 'Applied' with 'Applied-and-was-Rejected'.

Physics

Startling advances have been made in the field of sub-atomic physics by Rejects over the last decade, and the subject has consequently found a new popularity.

This has followed the prediction and imminent discovery of an entity, without charge, produced when an electron comes into collision with a photon but fails to be accepted into a higher quantum level. This has been termed a 'Rejecton'. It is believed to be neither a wave nor a particle. The existence of the Rejecton, although not subject to confirmation through experimental observation, is a theoretical certainty by virtue of its essential property, which is that it has no effect whatsoever on particles around it.

128

Chemistry

Tell anyone you are an Oxbridge Reject chemist, and you are bound to get a reaction. Although many Rejects find elements of the subject very dull, Chemistry does wonders for your social life. Chemists mix well and form lasting bonds with their colleagues.

But though the social side can be sublime, at some stage Reject Chemists must be practical and face up to the rigours of the course. Only in this way will the subject begin to crystallize.

Life Sciences

Life Sciences is a hybrid of Botany, Zoology, Psychology, Sociology and Anthropology.

This is a very useful course if you ever want to know who and what you are, who you are descended from, which of your neighbours are most closely related to you, which of your pets are most closely related to each other, which of your pets is most closely related to the man next-door, why the man next-door is a violent football hooligan, why he finds it amusing to break into your garden and pull up all your plants, which ones he pulled up last night, why the police have done nothing about him, and whether all his actions can be blamed upon television.

Engineering

Engineering is a constructive field, and Oxbridge Rejects considering a course in it should plan ahead to ensure that when they arrive at university they have already lain a firm foundation of related subjects on which they can build. For more concrete information, ask an engineer.

Medicine

The main disadvantage of studying medicine is having to remember Latin and Greek terms for every little bit of the body, from the top of the *cranium* down to the last *metatarsal*, and not forgetting the *diverticulum* off the *intestinium caecum*. (For further information – see *appendix*.)

The Reject at Work
A Report by Mrs Joan Bland,
Senior Careers Advisor,
The Oxbridge Reject Society

The choice of career is always difficult, and although Oxbridge Rejects are as likely as any to be forced to reconsider their chosen career in mid-course, it is nonetheless the first steps which are the most important. In this ever more competitive world, information is the key that will open doors. It is therefore vital that members have access to comprehensive and reliable datt on a wide range of careers.

The Careers Department exists to offer members advice and sympathy as they search for a field of employment in which they will excel. Over the years the Department has been greatly helped by members of the Society already employed in any given profession, and is always grateful to Rejects who are prepared to give up a little time to talk about their experiences. In particular the Department would like to hear from anyone working in the following areas, on which we have no files at present:

- Endoscopy
- Calligraphy
- Industry

Whilst contact with members of the Society already working in a given field can be invaluable in forming a better picture of the work entailed, the Careers Department would deny any accusations that this has led to the emergence of the so-called 'Old Reject Network'. Nonetheless the Department asks, as always, that all members of the Society currently in employment look favourably upon any application from a fellow Reject.

Finding the Right Job

Where to Start

Finding the right job is largely a matter of asking the right questions. A good one to start with is:

1. What do I want to do?

The first step in the great search for employment must be to decide what it is you want to do.

Over the years the Careers Department has compiled a list of the six jobs for which Oxbridge Rejects most often apply. They are:

- Chairman of the Bank of England
- Chief Conductor of the City of Birmingham Symphony Orchestra
- Editor of *Vogue*
- Chief Executive of the Coca-Cola Corporation
- Commander-in-Chief, British Army of the Rhine
- Vice Chancellor of Oxford University

Unfortunately in the jobs market demand often exceeds supply, and consequently there are no recorded instances of any members of the Society ever reaching any of these positions, either as a first job or indeed later in their careers. This shows that asking just one question may not be sufficient. It may also be useful to ask:

2. Are there any vacancies?

Although it will almost certainly restrict the options open to you, as a general principle you should apply only for positions that are not already filled. This is not an infallible rule. There is nearly always a Poet Laureate, for example, and if you really want the post you should not let this put you off. But it is often easier to get a job if there is a vacancy, and you should therefore look for the clues that identify such vacancies – such as job advertisements in newspapers.

Some areas of the economy are likely to offer more vacancies and better chances of promotion than others, and the Careers Department advises Rejects to concentrate their efforts on those industries that are enjoying rapid expansion, rather than those in terminal decline. For example, while there is little call these days for druids, the demand for astronauts has increased considerably over the last seven centuries.

But having decided that you want to be an opinion poll researcher, for example, and having identified it as an expanding profession, you must be sure to buy a clip-board, then stop yourself and ask the question, 'Could I do the job?'

3. Could I do the job?

It is important that you can answer this question by saying 'Yes'. Holding down a job that you cannot do can be very stressful. Too many Rejects take on highly-skilled careers, such as that of trapeze artist, only to find that they are losing their grip and that they have to let the job go.

Although you may not discover that you are unsuited to a job until you take it on, as a very rough guide you should look to your qualifications. These will help to direct you towards the type of career best suited to you, and indicate an appropriate level of entry.

If, for example, you want a job capping uncontrolled fires raging on oil rigs, but your only qualification is Spanish 'A' level, you should probably try to get some experience of the petro-chemical industry – and you might therefore consider sitting Chemistry GCSE.

But employers are not looking exclusively for academic qualifications. The more interest that you can show in your chosen occupation the better. You might also therefore think about joining your local Oil Rig Fire Extinguishing Society.

However, even having the ideal qualifications, and knowing that a particular job is the right one for you may not be enough in itself. You must also make employers notice you. The best way to do this is to apply for the job.

4. Have I applied for the job?

You may have heard from your friends of employers who say, 'Don't ring us – we'll ring you,' and you may have assumed from this that it is the employers who do the job hunting. Although they certainly do have a role to play in the recruitment process, the chances of a prospective employer getting in touch with you are increased considerably if you send them an application form.

Filling in these forms can be quite difficult, and is certainly not made any easier by the misleading wording used on some of them. Most importantly you should be aware that just because a company claims to be an equal opportunities employer, it does not necessarily mean that they will be looking to employ an equal number of Oxbridge Rejects and Oxbridge Graduates.

When completing the application form, try to bear in mind that the employers will be asking themselves not what they can offer you, but what you can offer them. Indeed, if you are really keen to get ahead it is something that you might consider asking yourself.

5. What can I offer an employer?

Although many Rejects will be reluctant to answer this question honestly, this is not a time for modesty. You should flaunt yourself, and, in particular, bear in mind that many employers will be impressed by your membership of the Society.

Oxbridge Rejects are highly sought after as employees because most companies are looking for two key characteristics in those whom they appoint. First, they do not want their new recruits to leave once their training is completed. Years of experience indicates that Rejects are so loyal that they are rarely approached by headhunters with talk of 'golden hellos' and 'offers they cannot refuse'.

Secondly, many interviewers feel threatened by the fact that they may, one day, find themselves in direct competition for promotion with their interviewees. Oxbridge Rejects are aware of this fact and are adept at giving the impression that the chance of them out-performing the interviewer can be classed as an acceptable risk.

Having answered all five questions, you will now be ready to enter your chosen profession. How well such a career suits you and how well you will perform can be judged, to some extent, by the analysis that follows of other members of the Society already working in the field.

Don't forget that if you ever want *any* advice or help with career matters, we at the Oxbridge Reject Careers Service are always here to assist you. It's your Careers Service, so use it. We are one of the most expensive Departments that the Society operates, so it is very important that the cost involved is seen to be justified.

You know where to find us.

The Careers Service

Opening times: 11.00–4.00, Tuesday to Friday; closed daily for lunch, 12.30–2.30; closed Tuesday morning for re-shelving of files; half day Wednesdays; staff training Thursdays, 11.15–12.15. Please note that the Senior Careers Advisor is not available on Fridays.

Oxbridge Reject Careers

The Department has compiled a report on a random selection of Reject occupations to help those who are about to enter the job market for the first time, for those who may be thinking of re-entering it, and for those who have been in it for a very long time indeed.

Postman
Although it is often assumed that a great many Oxbridge Rejects begin their working lives with the Post Office, this is in fact not the case. Remarkably few Rejects work in the postal sector, discouraged by the long and inconvenient hours.

International Statesman
The Careers Department has been unable to contact any Oxbridge Reject who has pursued a career in this field.

Communist Double Agent
This is not a job that the Careers Department recommends since there is no fixed career structure, retirement prospects are subject to last minute alterations and twice as much
134

paperwork is involved as for ordinary agents – some of which must be eaten. Consequently we do not stock the relevant application forms.

These objections aside, Oxbridge Rejects have been known to excel as Communist Double Agents. It is not widely known, for example, that – despite rumours to the contrary – the so-called 'Fifth Man' is a member of the Society, and has only avoided detection because it has always been supposed that he must have been recruited, like Burgess, Philby, Maclean and Blunt, whilst at Cambridge. This was indeed the case, with the difference that his recruitment took place whilst he was up at interview. He subsequently studied Art History elsewhere, having been rejected by Cambridge because his Russian was not good enough. He now lives happily in Sienna on the Via Pantaneto.

Accountancy

This remains one of the most popular careers for members of the Society, particularly those who have studied economics and mathematics. Accountancy firms are very keen to recruit Rejects because they are aware that few people fail more than one major set of exams in their lives. Although Reject accountants are usually bored by their work, it is seldom taxing, and they console themselves by overcharging enormously for their services.

Member of Parliament

To Rejects, the main attractions of becoming a Member of Parliament are that MPs are able to:
- appear on television
- classify the reading of newspapers as 'work'
- classify the writing of letters to newspapers as 'work'.

Oxbridge Rejects are particularly keen to be in Opposition where an already minimal workload is yet further reduced. When not in government one can say and do anything – however unconstructive – sure of the fact that it will have no effect whatsoever.

The Church

There are a great number of Reject clergy of all creeds and denominations throughout the world. But although Rejects

135

make good priests, rabbis and witch doctors, so far the top jobs have eluded them, and no Oxbridge Reject has yet become Archbishop of Canterbury, Pope, Spiritual Leader of the Islamic world, or Dalai Lama.

Within the Church of England, few Rejects have made it even as far as Bishop, probably because of the suspicion with which they are regarded by the Synod as a result of the Society's historical associations with the demise of Thomas à Becket.

The Monarchy

By far the easiest way to become a monarch is to be born into the profession – nepotism is not discouraged. Unfortunately the Careers Department cannot refer Rejects to any British monarch for further information as in this country no members of the Royal Family have been rejected by the Universities of Oxford or Cambridge – although a few may have come quite close.

Those considering a career in this field should be aware that life as a monarch is not as exciting as many people think; nor is it nearly as glamorous as, for example, a career in advertising.

Advertising

At present the Society is not well represented within the advertising industry, and this is a situation which the Careers Department has been endeavouring to remedy.

Two years ago, the Marketing Department launched, on our behalf, an advertising campaign targeted at the personnel departments of the top twenty advertising agencies. Marketing rejected creative work from the agency they had selected eighteen times before they finally accepted a bold, bright, dynamic, colourful, eye-catching, fun, lovable, powerful and racy campaign with the strapline: 'Reject Advertising – You Won't Regret It'. This went on trial in Tyne Tees, with two thirty-second spots on drive-time local radio and a half-page, colour, follow-up advertisement in *Awake!*, the region's Jehovah's Witness magazine.

Tracking studies have revealed, however, that unprompted recall amongst agency personnel directors was low. Following a review and a three-way pitch for the account, the incumbent agency was reappointed and the strategy has undergone a complete rethink. The new advertisement, with the strapline 'Reject Advertising – You Know It Makes Sense' is shortly to be trialed in the North of Scotland with three twenty-second spots on prime time local radio and two, quarter-page, colour advertisements in *Rejoice!*, the parish magazine of the Inner Hebrides.

Bus Driving

Following research into the economy carried out in conjunction with the CBI, the Careers Department has identified Bus Transport as a boom industry in the next decade. This has come about as a result of the growth in 'Park and Ride' services and the increasing introduction of small 'Hoppa' buses.

Public Relations

In recent years the Department has noted a considerable increase in the number of Rejects entering this profession. Consequently it recently compiled a questionnaire which it distributed to all members registered as working in this field, in order to try to establish what it is exactly that PRs do for a living. To date only one reply has been received. It was faxed to us last week and is reprinted below.

LATEST NEWS OF CHALLENGING ROLES IN PUBLIC RELATIONS

In this vigorous and thrusting field only the most dynamic and 'switched-on' Rejects can shine. The qualities which you must dispaly include total commitment, excellent writing ability, and strong communication skills. You will be in constant contact with the decision makers of the media world in a fast-moving and exciting environment.

Architecture

Architecture has been very popular with Oxbridge Rejects since the mid-50s.

Journalism

The best reason for becoming a journalist is that it considerably reduces your chances of having articles written about you in newspapers and magazines. Oxbridge Rejects excel in this expanding field because it is usually more important to report the inspired thoughts of others than to have any inspired thoughts oneself.

Teaching

Oxbridge Rejects make natural teachers because, unlike Oxbridge Graduates, they recognize that not all schoolwork is an 'absolute doddle'. This is a good place to start when imparting knowledge.

They are also not prone to confusing their pupils with unnecessary amounts of detail, having little inclination themselves to commit obscure facts to memory. Furthermore, Rejects are popular teachers because, just as their students are reluctant to do any more work than is strictly necessary, so they are disinclined to mark such work.

This is not to say that Rejects are not conscientious teachers, and many members of the Society who enter this profession make the most of their particular gift for understanding the workings of the non-academic mind.

Marketing

Those who work in marketing can be identified by their unusual interests and priorities. They enjoy nothing more than hours of discussion about biscuits, shampoos and pet foods, and are rarely happier than when visiting supermarkets to compare shelf sizes. When not discussing these topics, they amuse themselves by rubbishing their advertising agency and doubting whether their PR consultants deserve one tenth of the money that they pay them.

The Armed Forces

For patriotic reasons the Society used to be keen to limit the number of Rejects joining the Armed Forces. It is now recognized, however, that Rejects shine in all three Services.

They are attracted by the incentive that the more senior you get the less you have to do – and the more people you have to help you do it. Many Oxbridge Rejects have become very senior indeed.

The Oxbridge Reject Society

A career with the Oxbridge Reject Society is highly recommended. Of all the different careers covered in this report, a recent survey conducted by the Department indicated that those who work for the Society enjoy the most secure jobs, the shortest working weeks and the largest number of months of paid holiday. The financial rewards can also be attractive, and the Society operates an excellent pension scheme through the Treasury's Oxford and Cambridge Reject Widows' Mutual Benevolent Assurance and Pension Fund. Furthermore, promotion is not related to performance, or indeed, to anything else.

There are a wide range of posts available, some appointed and some elected. For further information contact the Senior Careers Advisor today (weekdays only; not Mondays or Fridays; not Tuesday mornings, not Wednesday afternoons, not Thursday mornings).

Banking

Financial rewards in banking are in inverse proportion to the number of hours of sleep which employees enjoy. In their twenties Oxbridge Rejects accept this fact and go for the money, but soon burn out and the emphasis switches to the sleep.

The Law

Rejects should be very certain that they wish to become lawyers because they will be expected to spend years preparing for a world in which all copies of the *All England Law Reports* have been mysteriously lost. This, at any rate, must be assumed to be the reason that lawyers are required to commit to memory all cases in which legal precedent has been set, from *Anns* v. *London Borough of Merton* [1977] 2 W.L.R. 1024, to *Yousoupoff* v. *Metro-Goldwyn-Mayer Pictures* [1934] 50 T.L.R. 581.

The Law is also the only profession in which time spent

calculating fees is chargeable. Because, in any case, the system of working out fees is almost entirely random, a career in Law can be extremely rewarding.

Oil Rig Fire Extinguishing
It is vital that Rejects entering this profession have the proper qualifications – those without them can get their fingers burnt.

Farming
Oxbridge Rejects have had a long association with innovation in farming techniques. Indeed, many Reject farmers had been in the habit of growing few or no crops long before the advent of the European Economic Community made such a practice highly profitable.

Trapeze Artistry
Although numbers in this profession are falling, a few Rejects do still reach the top of the ladder. But it is important when thinking about becoming a trapeze artist to be aware that by no means all reach the dizzying heights of the greatest Reject performers. For every one who succeeds there are a hundred who never really get into the swing of things, and either drop out or end up letting their colleagues down.

Many failed trapeze artists find themselves performing other circus roles: some get roped in to being escapologists; others have a shot at being a human cannonball; a few unfortunates try their hand at being lion tamers but soon find that they have bitten off more than they can chew.

Book Award Judging
There are some people who think that the judges of the Booker Prize, the Whitbread Prize, and the Nobel Prize for Literature are incompetents who could not spot literary talent if it fell out of the sky and hit them on the head, marked 'The Oxbridge Reject Society Prospectus'.

However, the Editors of this publication have asked the Careers Department to point out that it is their belief that such a view is absurd. It's nonsense. It's ridiculous. The judges are in fact doing an almost impossible job extremely well. Well done. Terrific. Bravo.

Rejects are, of course, entering new fields all the time, and the Careers Service tries quite hard to keep abreast of developments. If you would like information on any career not covered above, please write to the Senior Careers Advisor, enclosing a stamped, self-addressed A6 envelope, to the usual address. Please note that the Careers Department is extremely busy at all times, so you are advised not to expect a reply within twenty-eight days.

A Portrait of the Reject as Genius: The Achievements of the Great Oxbridge Rejects
by Jeremy Nuttington-Crisp, Esq

Jeremy Nuttington-Crisp is Senior Archivist to the Society and Director of the Oxbridge Reject Fine Art Commission. He is one of the Society's most distinguished scholars, and an eclectic and multi-disciplined *bellettrist*. He recently finished editing the *Dictionary of Reject Biography* (ORP, pp 29, £65), and this fact, combined with his lifelong interest in the Society, renders him peculiarly well-qualified to write on the subject of Reject achievements.

One could produce an entire book on the subject of the achievements of Oxbridge Rejects. Indeed, I recently have. Many, however, have doubted that it is a subject worthy of study, arguing that by their very nature Oxbridge Rejects are, in some undefined sense, non-achievers. I would like, here, to repudiate such a view.

To do true justice to the diverse and all-embracing advances which Oxbridge Rejects have made in every sphere – whether with pen or brush, with chisel or potter's wheel, with camera or sieve – it is essential that we first have a clear concept of what constitutes greatness.

Many critics have argued that a major achievement – a work of genius – is something absolute, existing outside the vacillations of tradition or the destructive onslaught of time. True genius, they would claim, reveals itself to the observer through some semi-spiritual intervention of the aesthetic.

But this is not, as it would seem, an absolute argument. Differences between aesthetic responses must render any accomplishment liable to a subjective interpretation, thereby debasing it. Thus the works of the nineteenth-century Reject composer Josiah Cartwright, regarded by some as the most sublime contribution to the repertoire for brass ensemble, might be viewed by non-lovers of colliery band music-making as a cacophonous hotch-potch of commonplace and repetitive marches.

A second contention is that genius is distinguished by the elapse of time. But how can this be so? For *Tempora mutantur et nos mutamur in illis*, and circumstance is not always the friend to one striving for greatness. Who can say which pre-eminent Greek philosophers now lie unadmired, their works lost during the passage of centuries? Like a man trapped in a cave, we can only speculate. For with every generation, what little we know of the past fades, like a priceless tapestry in bright sunlight, further into the dusk of anonymity.

Instead we must offer a new bench-mark for greatness; a scheme which allows for a broader appreciation of achievement. It is one's contention that true genius lies not in the recognition of the critic, nor in the respectability of endurance, but in the myriad cat's-cradle of other advances from which it is born.

To understand greatness, then, is to understand the climate from which it proceeds; the intellectual parents which nurture it and the sociological needs which it fulfills. Necessity may be the mother of invention; but inspiration is its great aunt.

Given, then, our new precept of genius, how can we assess the true wealth of achievements made by Oxbridge Rejects? How can we come to appreciate the many advances which Rejects have made in so many fields? The answer lies, surely, in knowing where to look. There are countless examples of Reject genius which have failed to be recognized as such, either because they have been made in an endeavour not normally associated with the pinnacles of human strivings, or because in the course of events they have been eclipsed by the achievements of others.

Nowhere is this more apparent than in Reject Art. We are taught to admire the magnificence and skill of Michelangelo's work on the ceiling of the Sistine Chapel, yet who stops to wonder at the very basis from which the art lover gazes? For anyone interested in Renaissance stonework the floor of the Sistine Chapel is a rare treat – a marvellous tapestry of

143

interlocking tiles, mirroring the splendour of the terrestrial firmament – and, significantly, the work of an Oxbridge Reject stonemason. Then again, what remains of the reputation enjoyed by the members of the twentieth-century Reject school of artists, the Squarists? Eclipsed by the Cubist movement, which developed out of the new boundaries established by this Reject School, the Squarists are today scarcely remembered by art historians or critics, who had always regarded their work as lacking in depth and dimensionality.

Reject literature, too, has never received the critical acclaim which it so richly deserves. One can cite numerous literary milestones, now published only by the Oxbridge Reject Press (in their splendid 'Reject Classics' series), which have been denied attention simply because they were subsequently eclipsed by the work of others. One thinks of Thomas Casterbridge's obscure novel 'Jude the Quite Shy'; George Endwell's apocalyptic '1983'; and, of course, the much-acclaimed 1965 modernist masterpiece 'Rosencrantz and Guildenstern are Unwell'.

Equally, one cannot overlook those pioneering Reject authors who produced work of unquestionable quality, but whose manuscripts were never accepted by a publishing house because they were felt to be ahead of their time. As a consequence these authors have never received the recognition that they deserve for preparing the ground for subsequent writers. In this category one must include the numerous works of Charlotte and Emily Stephenson, especially Emily's magnificent *Wuthering Areas of Above Average Altitude*; Charles Twist's *A Tale of Two Towns Created by Charter and Commonly Containing a Cathedral*; and Leo Ivanovitch's magnificent twelve-volume novel *Cross-border Conflict and Cessation of Strife*.

Most unjust of all are those examples of Reject endeavour which remain popular, but which are never attributed to their creator. This is perhaps most prevalent in the field of music. The example which most immediately springs to mind is that of Franz von Ludwig, an Oxbridge Reject and a remarkable *avant garde* composer of the late nineteenth century.

144

Ludwig's most noteworthy contribution to the repertoire, a short anthem employing a highly experimental and chromatic approach to its examination of the theme of order triumphing over chaos, is played more often than any other orchestral composition – indeed it is extremely rare that an opera or concert does not begin with his *Random Prelude without Conductor for Woodwind, Strings and Brass in A minor*. Perhaps we should be grateful to be given so many opportunities to hear this sublime work, but it is galling that Ludwig's visionary deconstructionist composition has never been attributed to him.

In the case of another Oxbridge Reject composer, Sergei Mikhail Boris Ilyich Rostrokovsky of Novgarod, the fate of his life's work has been still more unhappy. Commissioned, at the age of sixteen, to compose a new Russian National Anthem, Rostrokovsky spent forty-two years completing the piece to his satisfaction, utterly neglecting all other work during this period. The anthem was to have been premièred at the Winter Palace in Petrograd, on a March evening in 1917, but for reasons beyond the control of the orchestra, *God Save The Tsar* was never played. All copies were lost in the revolutionary struggles of the next few months, and – heartbroken – Rostrokovsky never composed another bar of music. Such is the tragedy of genius.

From the film industry's earliest years, Oxbridge Rejects have also been very active in cinematic art. Without exception, however, they have been greeted by that rare combination of both critical and popular apathy, which has been so characteristic of the response to Reject Art in general.

One of the earliest luminaries of the burgeoning British cinema was Alfred Leighton, an Oxbridge Reject film cameraman whose career spanned nearly ten years both with British Gaumont at Elstree, and later with Ealing Films. As well as being a supreme technician, Leighton was also a great innovator. It was he who devised the apparatus for rolling titles, which was first used for the credits on Leighton's last film, the classic comedy *Mr Bunting Goes West*. This marvellous invention made it possible for the name of everyone involved in the making of the film to be displayed swiftly, with the result that for the first time gaffers, key grips and best boys were credited. Ironically, owing to an oversight on the part of the producer, Leighton's was the one name not included in the film's credits.

Perhaps the most important figure in the modern genre known as Reject Film is David 'Jack' Spratt, the British writer, director and cinematic theorist. Although Spratt has, to date, completed over twenty films, none of this considerable body of work has ever received a general release. Perhaps his finest – and significantly his shortest – film, *Idyll*, deals with the experiences of a pair of deaf, mute twins applying to Oxford in the late 20s to read Modern Languages. Based on a short story by the director's wife, and filmed entirely without sound on Super 8mm, this astonishing masterpiece is both a searing indictment of prejudice and class-hatred during the inter-war period, and an amusing, light-hearted romp.

It is clear that there are many examples of Reject achievement which have never been appreciated as such by the wider populus. But viewed within the context of these artists' intentions, the social and intellectual circles in which these great Rejects moved, and the times in which they lived, should not all these Rejects be recognized as the geniuses they truly were?

Da Vinci's plans for a helicopter were originally seen as the insane jottings of an old man – it is only recently that the breadth of his vision has been celebrated. Is it not, therefore, inevitable that, as we come to reassess our precepts of genius, many great Rejects will come to be lauded for their achievements? Who can doubt that in a few years, no guidebook to Rome will omit an appreciation of the floor of the Sistine Chapel, no modern art gallery will be without its own example of the 'Squarist' *oeuvre*, and no cinematic retrospective complete without a contribution from David Spratt?

To return to our original contention, it can be seen that far from being non-achievers, Oxbridge Rejects have enriched every aspect of our nation's culture and heritage: they have given us writers and artists, musicians and cinematographers, inventors and stonemasons whose contributions defy assessment.

146

We must therefore consider the common force that has driven Rejects onward into every field of human endeavour; we must inquire more deeply into the creative Reject urge that has been responsible for so much of note.

The nature of this urge, lies, one fancies, in the very process of rejection that unites us all; the experience, shared by all members of the Society, of failing to be admitted to Oxbridge. Whilst others spend their lives furtively glancing over their metaphorical shoulders, terrified lest failure might – as in the children's game of Grandmother's Footsteps – be creeping up on them, Rejects know no such anxieties. They have met failure and rejection relatively early in their lives, and have come to regard them as old acquaintances, who come frequently to visit.

In addition, Oxbridge Rejects have shared the experience of not studying at Oxford or Cambridge. This too is important. Three or four years at Oxford or Cambridge must surely affect a person's perceptions of success. Whilst Rejects leave university and consider themselves to be successful if they achieve a modicum of comfort and contentment and can eat quite regularly, Oxbridge graduates seem to feel an insuperable urge to make enormous piles of money, publish shelves of books and appear on television every night.

Furthermore, it is impossible as a student at either Oxford or Cambridge to be unaware of the contributions that graduates of these great universities have made in every field: Milton, Keynes, Waugh, Graves, Swift, Carr, Gray, Rhodes, Wilde, Oates, Bacon, Sandwich – the list is endless. But such is not the case at those universities attended by Rejects. The majority of students at these institutions would struggle to name more than a couple of notable graduates.

Have we then uncovered the crux of what sets the Reject artist apart from all others? Have we discovered the subtle thread which links Oxbridge Rejection with supreme creative achievement? Can we in truth claim that the very process of failing Oxbridge fosters the perfect climate in which genius may blossom? By failing Oxbridge and studying for a degree elsewhere, members of the Society are confronted with the need to cope with failure and rejection, acquire by default a modest view of success, and are spared the stifling pressure of feeling obliged to live up to famous predecessors.

As Director of the Reject Fine Art Commission, I am aware that there are members of the Society who are keen to see greater recognition for Reject endeavours in all fields of art and innovation. It has even been suggested that the Commission should institute an annual Oxbridge Reject Festival of Art. The Commission's response has always been that individual Reject artists do indeed deserve greater recognition for their work in all its diversity. However, a Reject festival, by its very nature, would glorify Reject Art not just individually, but also collectively. As such, any specifically 'Reject' festival would result in irreversible damage to the heritage that it sought to promote, and the climate of creativity which Rejects have enjoyed in the past would be destroyed forever.

Meddle with this climate and the effects would be disastrous. No longer could Rejects believe that they were without artistic forebears with whom to compete. The whole Reject perception of success would be replaced by brazen, hard-nosed ambition. Aspiring artists would look upon Rejection from Oxbridge as a passport to recognition and success, never learning to cope with criticism and failure.

The state of Oxbridge Rejection is unique, and we must work hard to preserve it. Much of this task, in the field of arts appreciation, falls to the Reject Fine Art Commission, which endeavours to protect the conditions in which so many Reject achievements have bloomed. It is a tribute to the Commission's efforts, and to those of the Society itself over the last 700 years, that Reject creativity as a collective art-form has yet to be noticed.

J. N-C,
Via Panteneto,
Sienna

Oxbridge Reassessed

Earlier in the year, the editors of the Prospectus received the following letter from Mr Gavin Trent, an Oxbridge Reject currently pursuing postgraduate studies in Chemistry at the University of Keele.

Whilst the ediors would like to state that the letter does not necessarily reflect their own views, or those of the Society, it is reprinted here at the express request of Mr Trent.

An Open Letter to the Governors
of the Oxbridge Reject Society

There recently came into my possession a copy of last year's oxbridge reject society annual report and accounts. Although I had never previously heard of the oxbridge reject society, I discovered on reading through its annual report that I was considered to be a member. I wish to openly state here that, having read this document, I now disassociate myself completely from your society.

In a so-called democratic country it is unacceptable that any organisation should claim to automatically recruit members, without first seeking to establish whether individuals wish to join. I therefore regard your suggestion that I am a part of your offensive society as both an insult and an infringement of my basic human rights.

Your annual report was one of the most repellent documents which I have ever read. The only reason, in fact, that I did read it at all was in an attempt to find some details about the procedure for opting out of society membership. That you omitted to include such information is doubtless no accident, and you probably assumed, in your smugness, that

149

all those who you so casually label 'rejects' would be too apathetic to complain about your negligence. Well you were wrong. I, for a start, am not too apathetic, and I wish here to openly state my utter contempt for your contemptible society, and to abundantly make it clear that I wish to immediately resign my membership.

There are a number of reasons for this. Firstly, while reading the treasurer's report I was appalled to discover that the society has a policy of making payments to oxford and cambridge universities. Although when I took oxbridge I had been made blind to the fact, I can now see that these institutions are nothing more than entrenched bastions of the bourgeois intelligensia, luxuriating in a cesspool of complacency of their own making, masquerading under the tainted disguise of rarified academe. Whether or not you are aware of it, your subsidies are being used to deliberately perpetuate this status quo, and as such the oxbridge reject society represents a significant barrier to immediate social reforms culminating in a radical emasculation of the most cancerous elements within our nation.

What, in any case, is the justificaton for such payments? Both oxford and cambridge are obscenely rich in comparison to all other universities. Yet what do they actually achieve that is so deserving of society funds? The answer is nothing.

In last year's report the treasurer described oxford and cambridge as 'those fine seats of learning upon which the Society places such reliance'. He later refers to the 'important work of our two leading universities'. Clearly the oxbridge reject society is as thoroughly imbued with the spirit of sycophantic and unjustified admiration for oxford and cambridge as the rest of our class-ridden society. Indeed the fact that in your annual report you think that the 'Universities' and 'Graduates' of 'Oxford' and 'Cambridge' deserve capital letters is just a small indication of the pathetic toadying that is evident on every page of this nauseating document.

Let me put the record straight: oxford and cambridge are not 'our two leading Universities' but merely our two oldest, and their reputations and claims to success are based on privilege and wealth rather than on equality. As such they

150

are guilty of more far-reaching damage to our society than even the royal family, the aristocracy and the public schools which collectively control them. It is oxbridge more than any other self-perpetuating oligarchy which has been responsible for the unjustified pre-eminence of the pre-eminent and the continued repression of the repressed.

The fact is that oxford and cambridge are clinging so desperately to the past that they have no time for anything of relevance to the modern world. The oxbridge obsession with the study of dead languages, ancient civilisations and discarded ideas is a shameful waste of resources. None of this is of any use – or interest – to those who do not waste their lives wearing ridiculous gowns, drinking port and eating swans. By teaching only as they themselves were taught, oxbridge so-called academics merely encourage misguided students to specialise in such obscure subjects that they are left unqualified to do anything except teach at oxford or cambridge.

For too long the ordinary citizens of this country have been deliberately brainwashed into believing that graduates of oxford and cambridge are in some way superior human beings, better qualified to run this nation, and deserving of our unqualified respect and deep-felt gratitude. Your subsidies to oxbridge would be a little easier to stomach if this *were* the case. But a quick look at the achievements of oxbridge graduates proves otherwise.

Although oxbridge graduates are only too happy to conceitedly point to the influential positions which they and their predecessors have reached in this country as evidence of their superiority, this is the wrong criteria to judge them on. After all, it was they who created the system, so it is not surprising that they continue to dominate it. To assess the achievements of those from oxbridge we must therefore look not to their positions of authority, but examine how badly they perform in such positions.

To our economy, oxbridge graduates have given monetarist and keynesian theories, but have refused to decide which is best. The instability caused by the continuous switching between the two has been instrumental in destroying this country's economic system. Our industrial base has crumbled,

151

we have fallen behind all our competitors, and I notice that the price of roll-your-own papers has just gone up again. But not everyone has suffered equally in this chaos: the manipulation of the economy by oxbridge graduates has made them and their old colleges rich – at the expense of everyone else.

To our political system, they have contributed prime minister after prime minister. All have been disastrous: either incompetent leaders with hopeless ideas, or hopeless leaders with incompetent ideas. In world affairs, we have had to watch as bungling by oxbridge graduates has lost us an empire won by others, destroyed our film industry, and involved us in two world wars – fought solely to protect the interests of the oxbridge élite. And at what cost to the universities of oxford and cambridge? How many bombs were actually dropped on oxford and cambridge during these two wars? Not very many at all, I bet.

The media also deserves a mention. Those oxbridge graduates who enter this profession seem to lack a vital quality for the job: an understanding of the relative importance of events, reflected in the attention apportioned to them. Who cares which University wins the varsity match? Why should they be allowed so many teams on 'University Challenge'? Why should the whole country be forced to watch the boat race?

Is it not time to ask why we allow an oxbridge-dominated media, seemingly unaware that there are more than two universities in this country, to pander to its own shameless whims? Is it not time that we elected politicians who have never attended these two bastions of privilege and who can therefore truly represent us? Is it not time that we forced the City fat-cats, who wantonly exploit oxbridge economics, to eat humble pie?

Oxbridge graduates have failed Britain at every turn and on every front. The only reason that we have been blind to this fact is that they have brainwashed us all into accepting a system of intolerable inequality. They have basked in their unjustified glory, cushioned by ceaseless, unjustified praise from their old university 'chums'.

We are endlessly told that we are too stupid to understand the complexities of the 'real world', and led to believe that only oxbridge 'types' can see what is good for us. And who

152

has been telling us this? The answer is transparently obvious – it is the oxbridge 'types' themselves: the politicians, the academics, the historians, the commentators, the judges, the clergy, the journalists, the teachers, all those in their pay, and – worst of all – the oxbridge reject society itself. They dare to claim that we have been well led, that wars are inevitable, that the economy is in good shape – even that roll-your-own papers are still relatively inexpensive.

You would think that all this failure would make oxbridge graduates pretty humble. Not a bit of it. However you look at it, humility and oxbridge graduation are worlds apart. It's high time that they met. The oxbridge élite must be made to realise what it has done, and accept that it has no option but to stand down, leaving the reins of power in more capable hands.

If the oxbridge élite does not accept this challenge and relinquish power voluntarily then at last this society of yours will have found a proper role to play. Finally it can live up to its name and reject oxbridge. Together we must fight for a better and more just society, free from antiquated and divisive distinctions based on class, education and football.

I call upon the oxbridge reject society to set up a protest group committed to immediate and ruthless action. We must smash the bastion of privilege that is oxbridge. We must force the two universities to their knees, up against the wall with their tails between their legs. We must bring to justice the parasitical flunkies who hide within these loathsome institutions. We must end the tyranny of our overfed oppressors.

To this end, all bridges in oxford and cambridge must be seized by force, and passage restricted to those who can prove that they have never had any dealings whatsoever with the universities. This will have three effects: it will utterly paralyse both universities; it will reduce traffic congestion; and it will provide members of the society with an opportunity to revisit these attractive towns.

In the meantime, we must impose hard-hitting sanctions on the anachronistic, outdated and archaic oxbridge system. In line with this, from today I personally will be boycotting all exports from oxford and cambridge: I will not be going on their diet, I will not be looking up words in their dictionaries, and I will not be eating their marmalade.

I call upon all members of the society to join me on this crusade. Together we can put the Reject back into the oxbridge reject society.

Gavin Trent

The Membership Secretary writes:

Dear Mr Trent,

Thank you for you kind enquiry, which I forwarded to myself, in my capacity as Prospectus Editor.

I would like to raise two points:

First, you may like to know that payments made by the Society to the Universities of Oxford and Cambridge have, at present, been halted.

Secondly, may I draw your attention to the fact that there is indeed a method of 'opting out' of the Oxbridge Reject Society, although the scheme is not operated by the Society itself. To this end, I would be happy to forward to you details of Colleges at the Universities of Oxford or Cambridge, which would, I feel sure, be pleased to consider your application.

Postscript

The Society's Marketing Department, in association with the Membership Secretary, is proud to announce that the Oxbridge Reject Tie and Brooch are now available to members of the Society.

Many of the Society's officers have been involved in the production of these useful and fashionable accessories, and every care has been taken to ensure that they are perfectly designed to help Oxbridge Rejects recognize one another.

No less than eighteen designs were put forward by Jeremy Nuttington-Crisp of the Reject Fine Art Commission before finally one was accepted. This is based on a heraldic crest, dated from the fourteenth century, discovered in our archive.

Dr Olivia Pegge, of the Statistics Department, conducted exhaustive research amongst members to help calculate the most desirable length for the Tie, and the ideal water-resistance for the Brooch.

Once a prototype of each had been produced, the Genetic Engineering Department generously volunteered a chimpanzee to test the Tie for durability, whilst the Brooch underwent performance analysis in a wind tunnel constructed specifically for the experiment by the Maintenance Department.

Having passed these controlled laboratory trials with flying colours, both products were subjected to extensive field tests by Steve Crozier, Society Universities Rep. who drove 11,500 miles wearing the Tie, and with the Brooch in his glove compartment.

Once a minor teething problem with creasing of the prototype Tie had been ironed out, and the cause of occasional difficulties with attaching the Brooch had been pinpointed, both went into production.

All those involved in the project would like to record their thanks to Arthur Botherington, Chairman of Governors, who offered constant encouragement and who has promised to buy a Tie for himself and a Brooch for his wife Muriel.

To date, the Requisitioning Department has placed our largest single order. At Christmas, the Department will be distributing Ties and Brooches to every Society employee as a surprise gift.

The Fundraising Department has expressed their delight with the gift of ten Ties and Brooches. The donation will do much to help the Department reach their Appeal target of £470 million. At the Summer Fête there are plans to set aside half of the Ties and Brooches for raffle prizes, whilst the remainder will be used for the Three-Legged Race and the ever-popular Pinning the Tail on the Donkey.

Dr Kurt Gunther, Consultant Psychologist to the Society, has recently published a short article: 'The Sociological Evidence for the Wearing of Such Badges of Allegiance as Evidence of an Externalization of Feelings of Loyalty.' Six copies of the paper have been placed in the Society Library and are available from the Very Short Loan section (which is situated just behind the Swedish Board Games of the Inter-War Period section).

Financial constraints permitting, the Space Programme hopes to be able to include both a Tie and a Brooch in their forthcoming space probe to the furthest reaches of the Milky Way. They are currently assessing the quantity of extra fuel which will be required for the probe to reach exit velocity.

In a recent speech announcing the Reject Awards for Industry, Ms Alison Clare BA Hons (oxon) MBA (Harv), Administrative Supervisor, referred to the project as 'A major triumph for the Society and an example to many of us. The production of the Oxbridge Reject Tie and Brooch has shown what can be achieved through determination, hard work, and a little realism. It also demonstrates how measures introduced by the Central Policy Review Committee have resulted in yet another success.'

Information about the Tie and Brooch can be obtained by sending details of your name and address to the Membership Secretary, and in order to avoid any disruption to the reliable workings of the post room, all enquiries should be clearly addressed to:

The Membership Secretary,
The Oxbridge Reject Society,
PO Box 1668,
London W8 7NJ.

In responding to these enquiries, the Membership Secretary promises quite uncharacteristic efficiency and rapidity.

Acknowledgements

The editors are very grateful to the following for their help in producing the Prospectus:

AWG; Jane Carr; Paul Micou; Philip Goodhart; William de Gale; Gareth Thomas; Leo Daley; Charles Mason; William Goodhart; Rod; Eilidh Fursman; Dr Kurt Gunther; David and Beccy Goodhart; Candida Ross-Macdonald; the Librarian of Rugby School; the Universities of Oxford and Cambridge; Rufus Stilgoe; Shipton Industries; Mandarin; Alan Sugar; the Association of British Trapeze Artists; and the staff of the Scarsdale Arms.

A Selected List of Humour Available from Mandarin

While every effort is made to keep prices low, it is sometimes necessary to increase prices at short notice. Mandarin Paperbacks reserves the right to show new retail prices on covers which may differ from those previously advertised in the text or elsewhere.

The prices shown below were correct at the time of going to press.

☐	7493 0159 7	**The Complete Fawlty Towers**	John Cleese and Connie Booth	£4.99
☐	7493 0178 3	**The Common Years**	Jilly Cooper	£3.99
☐	417 05370 3	**Supermen and Superwomen**	Jilly Cooper	£2.95
☐	7493 0252 6	**Turn Right at the Spotted Dog**	Jilly Cooper	£2.95
☐	7493 0138 4	**The Secret Diary of Adrian Mole Aged 13¾**	Sue Townsend	£2.99
☐	7493 0222 4	**The Growing Pains of Adrian Mole**	Sue Townsend	£2.99
☐	7493 0020 5	**Pratt of the Argus**	David Nobbs	£3.99
☐	7493 0097 3	**Second From Last in the Sack Race**	David Nobbs	£3.50

All these books are available at your bookshop or newsagent, or can be ordered direct from the publisher. Just tick the titles you want and fill in the form below.

Mandarin Paperbacks, Cash Sales Department, PO Box 11, Falmouth, Cornwall TR10 9EN.

Please send cheque or postal order, no currency, for purchase price quoted and allow the following for postage and packing:

UK   80p for the first book, 20p for each additional book ordered to a maximum charge of £2.00.

BFPO   80p for the first book, 20p for each additional book.

Overseas   £1.50 for the first book, £1.00 for the second and 30p for each additional book
including Eire   thereafter.

NAME (Block letters) ....

ADDRESS ....

....

....